Data Science Live Book

Pablo Casas

January 2019

Contents

Preface

Paperback & Kindle at Amazon

This book is now available at Amazon. **Check it out!**[1] 📄🚀.

Link to the black & white version, also available on full-color. It can be shipped to over 100 countries. 🌏

Why this book?

The book will facilitate the understanding of common issues when data analysis and machine learning are done.

Building a predictive model is as difficult as one line of R code:

```
my_fancy_model = randomForest(target ~ var_1 + var_2,
  my_complicated_data)
```

---
[1] https://www.amazon.com/dp/9874269049

That's it.

But, data has its dirtiness in practice. We need to sculp it, just like an artist does, to expose its information in order to find answers (and new questions).

There are many challenges to solve, some data sets requiere more *sculpting* than others. Just to give an example, random forest does not accept empty values, so what to do then? Do we remove the rows in conflict? Or do we transform the empty values into other values? **What is the implication**, in any case, to *my* data?

Despite the empty values issue, we have to face other situations such as the extreme values (outliers) that tend to bias not only the predictive model itself, but the interpretation of the final results. It's common to "try and guess" *how* the predictive model considers each variable (ranking best variables), and what the values that increase (or decrease) the likelihood of some event to happening (profiling variables) are.

Deciding the **data type** of the variables may not be trivial. A categorical variable *could be* numerical and viceversa, depending on the context, the data, and the algorithm itself (some of which only handle one data type). The conversion also has its own implications in *how the model sees the variables*.

It is a book about data preparation, data analysis and machine learning. Generally in literature, data preparation is not as popular as the creation of machine learning models.

The journey towards learning

The book has a highly practical approach, and tries to demonstrate what it states. For example, it says: *"Variables work in groups."*, and then you'll find a code that supports the idea.

3

Practically all chapters can be copy-pasted and be replicated by the reader to draw their own conclusions. Even more, whenever possible the code or script proposed (in R language) was thought generically, so it could be used in real scenarios, whether research or work.

The book's seed was the `funModeling` *R* library which started having a didactical documentation that quickly turned it into this book. Didactical because there is a difference between using a simple function that plots histograms to profile the target variable (`cross_plot`), and the explanation of how to get to semantical conclusions. The intention is to learn the inner concept, so you can *export that knowledge* to other languages, such as Python, Julia, etc.

This book, as well as the development of a data project, is not linear. The chapters are related among them. For example, the **missing values** chapter can lead to the **cardinality reduction in categorical variables**. Or you can read the **data type** chapter and then change the way you deal with missing values.

You'll find references to other websites so you can expand your study, *this book is just another step in the learning journey.*

Is this book for me? Will I understand it?

If you already are in the Data Science field, probably you don't think so. You'll pick the code you need, copy-paste it if you like, and that's it.

But if you are starting a data science career, you'll face a common problem in education: *To have answers to the questions that have not been made.*

For sure you will get closer to the data science world. All the code is well commented so you don't even need to be a programmer. This is the challenge of this book, to try and be friendly when reading, using logic, common sense and intuition.

Programming language

You could learn some R but it can be tough to learn directly from this book. If you want to learn R programming, there are other books or courses specialized in programming.

Time for next section.

Will machines and artificial intelligence rule the world?

Although it is true that computing power is being increased exponentially, the machines rebellion is far from happening today.

This book tries to expose common issues when creating and handling predictive models. Not a free lunch. There is also a relationship to *1-click solutions* and voilà! The predictive system is running and deployed. All the data preparation, transformations, table joins, timing considerations, tuning, *etc* is solved in one step.

Perhaps it is. Indeed as time goes by, there are more robust techniques that help us automatize tasks in predictive modeling. But just in case, it'd be a good practice not to trust blindly in black-box solutions without knowing, for example, how the system *picks up the best variables, what the inner procedure to validate the model is, how it deals with extremes or rare values*, among other topics covered in this book.

If you are evaluating some machine learning platform, some issues stated in this book can help you to decide the best option. Trying to *unbox the black-box*.

It's tough to have a solution that suits all the cases. Human intervention

is crucial in order to have a successful project. Rather than worry about machines, the point is *what the use of this technology will be.* Technology is *innocent.* It is the data scientist who sets the inputs and gives the model the needed target to learn. Patterns will emerge, and some of them could be harmful for many people. We have to be aware of the final objective, like in any other technologies.

> The machine is made by man, and it is what man does with it.

(Original quote in Spanish: "La maquina la hace el hombre, y es lo que el hombre hace con ella.")

By Jorge Drexler (musician, actor and doctor). Extracted from the song "Guitarra y vos".

Maybe, could this be the difference between **machine learning** and **data science**? A machine that learns vs. a human being doing science with data?

An open question.

What do I need to start?

In general terms, time and patience. Most of the concepts are independent from the language, but when a technical example is required it is done in **R language**[2], (R version 3.5.1 (2018-07-02)).

The book uses the following libraries, (between parenthesis it's the package version):

```
## funModeling (1.6.8), dplyr (0.7.6), Hmisc (4.1.1)
## reshape2 (1.4.3), ggplot2 (3.0.0), caret (6.0.80)
## minerva (1.4.7), missForest (1.4), gridExtra (2.3)
```

---

[2]https://cloud.r-project.org

```
## mice (3.1.0), Lock5Data (2.8), corrplot (0.84)
## RColorBrewer (1.1.2), infotheo (1.2.0)
```

The package `funModeling` was the origin of this book; it started as a set of functions to help the data scientist in their *daily* tasks. Now its documentation has evolved into this book ♥!

Install any of these by doing: `install.packages("PACKAGE_NAME")`.

The recommended IDE is **Rstudio**[3].

This book, both in pdf and web format, was created with Rstudio, using the incredible Bookdown[4].

It's all free and open-source, Bookdown, R, Rstudio and this book ☺

Hope you enjoy it!

How can I contact you? ✉

If you want to say *hello*, contribute by telling that some part is not well explained, suggest a new topic or share some good experience you had applying any concept explained here, you are welcome to drop me an email at:

pcasas.biz (at) gmail.com. I'm constantly learning so it's nice to exchange knowledge and keep in touch with other colleagues.

- Twitter[5]
- Linkedin[6]
- Github[7]
- Data Science Heroes Blog[8]

---

[3]https://www.rstudio.com/products/rstudio/download/
[4]https://bookdown.org/yihui/bookdown/
[5]https://twitter.com/pabloc__ds
[6]https://www.linkedin.com/in/pcasas
[7]https://github.com/pablo14
[8]http://blog.datascienceheroes.com

Also, you can check the **Github** repositories for both, the book and
`funModeling`, so you can report bugs, suggestions, new ideas, etc:

- funModeling[9]
- Data Science Live Book[10]

Acknowledgements

Special thanks to my mentors in this data world, Miguel Spindiak and
Marcelo Ferreyra.

Book technical reviewer: Pablo Seibelt (aka The Sicarul)[11] ✘ . Thank
you for your sincere and selfless help.

The art cover was made by: Bárbara Muñoz[12].

This book is dedicated to *The Nobodies*[13], a short story written by
Eduardo Galeano.

Book's information

First published at: livebook.datascienceheroes.com[14].

Licensed under Attribution-NonCommercial-ShareAlike 4.0 International[15].

ISBN: 978-987-42-5911-0 (eBook version).

---
[9]https://github.com/pablo14/funModeling
[10]https://github.com/pablo14/data-science-live-book
[11]https://www.linkedin.com/in/pabloseibelt
[12]https://www.linkedin.com/in/barbaramercedes/
[13]https://holywaters.wordpress.com/2011/12/08/los-nadiesthe-nobodies-by-eduardo-galeano
[14]http://livebook.datascienceheroes.com
[15]https://creativecommons.org/licenses/by-nc-sa/4.0/

1 Exploratory Data Analysis

Listening to the numbers :)

1.1 Profiling, The voice of the numbers

"The voice of the numbers" – a metaphor by Eduardo Galeano[16]. Writer and novelist.

The data we explore could be like Egyptian hieroglyphs without a correct interpretation. Profiling is the very first step in a series of

---

[16]https://en.wikipedia.org/wiki/Eduardo_Galeano

iterative stages in the pursuit of finding what the data want to tell us, if we are patient enough to listen.

This chapter will cover, with a few functions, a complete data profiling. This should be the entry step in a data project, where we start by knowing the correct data types and exploring distributions in numerical and categorical variables.

It also focuses on the extraction of semantic conclusions, which is useful when writing a report for non-technical people.

What are we going to review in this chapter?

- **Dataset health status:**
    - Getting metrics like total rows, columns, data types, zeros, and missing values
    - How each of the previous items impacts on different analysis
    - How to quickly filter and operate on (and with) them, to clean the data
- **Univariate analysis in categorical variable:**
    - Frequency, percentage, cumulative value, and colorful plots
- **Univariate analysis with numerical variables:**
    - Percentile, dispersion, standard deviation, mean, top and bottom values
    - Percentile vs. quantile vs. quartile
    - Kurtosis, skewness, inter-quartile range, variation coefficient
    - Plotting distributions
    - Complete **case study** based on *"Data World"*, data preparation, and data analysis

Functions summary review in the chapter:

- `df_status(data)`: Profiling dataset structure
- `describe(data)`: Numerical and categorical profiling (quantitative)
- `freq(data)`: Categorical profiling (quantitative and plot).

- `profiling_num(data)`: Profiling for numerical variables (quantitative)
- `plot_num(data)`: Profiling for numerical variables (plots)

Note: `describe` is in the `Hmisc` package while remaining functions are in `funModeling`.

1.1.1 Dataset health status

The quantity of zeros, NA, Inf, unique values as well as the data type may lead to a good or bad model. Here's an approach to cover the very first step in data modeling.

First, we load the **funModeling** and **dplyr** libraries.

```
# Loading funModeling!
library(funModeling)
library(dplyr)
data(heart_disease)
```

1.1.1.1 Checking missing values, zeros, data type, and unique values

Probably one of the first steps, when we get a new dataset to analyze, is to know if there are missing values (**NA** in **R**) and the data type.

The `df_status` function coming in **funModeling** can help us by showing these numbers in relative and percentage values. It also retrieves the infinite and zeros statistics.

```
# Profiling the data input
df_status(heart_disease)
```

	variable	q_zeros	p_zeros	q_na	p_na	q_inf	p_inf	type	unique
1	age	0	0.00	0	0.00	0	0	integer	41
2	gender	0	0.00	0	0.00	0	0	factor	2
3	chest_pain	0	0.00	0	0.00	0	0	factor	4
4	resting_blood_pressure	0	0.00	0	0.00	0	0	integer	50
5	serum_cholestoral	0	0.00	0	0.00	0	0	integer	152
6	fasting_blood_sugar	258	85.15	0	0.00	0	0	factor	2
7	resting_electro	151	49.83	0	0.00	0	0	factor	3
8	max_heart_rate	0	0.00	0	0.00	0	0	integer	91
9	exer_angina	204	67.33	0	0.00	0	0	integer	2
10	oldpeak	99	32.67	0	0.00	0	0	numeric	40
11	slope	0	0.00	0	0.00	0	0	integer	3
12	num_vessels_flour	176	58.09	4	1.32	0	0	integer	4
13	thal	0	0.00	2	0.66	0	0	factor	3
14	heart_disease_severity	164	54.13	0	0.00	0	0	integer	5
15	exter_angina	204	67.33	0	0.00	0	0	factor	2
16	has_heart_disease	0	0.00	0	0.00	0	0	factor	2

Figure 1: Dataset health status

- q_zeros: quantity of zeros (p_zeros: in percent)
- q_inf: quantity of infinite values (p_inf: in percent)
- q_na: quantity of NA (p_na: in percent)
- type: factor or numeric
- unique: quantity of unique values

1.1.1.2 Why are these metrics important?

- **Zeros**: Variables with **lots of zeros** may not be useful for modeling and, in some cases, they may dramatically bias the model.
- **NA**: Several models automatically exclude rows with NA (**random forest** for example). As a result, the final model can be biased due to several missing rows because of only one variable. For example, if the data contains only one out of 100 variables with 90% of NAs, the model will be training with only 10% of the original rows.
- **Inf**: Infinite values may lead to an unexpected behavior in some functions in R.

12

- **Type**: Some variables are encoded as numbers, but they are codes or categories and the models **don't handle them** in the same way.
- **Unique**: Factor/categorical variables with a high number of different values (~30) tend to do overfitting if the categories have low cardinality (**decision trees,** for example).

1.1.1.3   Filtering unwanted cases

The function **df_status** takes a data frame and returns a *status table* that can help us quickly remove features (or variables) based on all the metrics described in the last section. For example:

Removing variables with a *high number* of zeros

```
# Profiling the Data Input
my_data_status = df_status(heart_disease,
  print_results = F)


# Removing variables with 60% of zero values
vars_to_remove = filter(my_data_status, p_zeros >
  60) %>% .$variable
vars_to_remove
```

```
## [1] "fasting_blood_sugar" "exer_angina"
## [3] "exter_angina"
```

```
# Keeping all columns except the ones present in
# 'vars_to_remove' vector
heart_disease_2 = select(heart_disease,
  -one_of(vars_to_remove))
```

Ordering data by percentage of zeros

```
arrange(my_data_status, -p_zeros) %>% select(variable,
  q_zeros, p_zeros)
```

```
##                        variable q_zeros p_zeros
## 1        fasting_blood_sugar     258   85.15
## 2                 exer_angina     204   67.33
## 3                exter_angina     204   67.33
## 4           num_vessels_flour     176   58.09
## 5     heart_disease_severity     164   54.13
## 6              resting_electro     151   49.83
## 7                     oldpeak      99   32.67
## 8                         age       0    0.00
## 9                      gender       0    0.00
## 10                 chest_pain       0    0.00
## 11     resting_blood_pressure       0    0.00
## 12          serum_cholestoral       0    0.00
## 13             max_heart_rate       0    0.00
## 14                      slope       0    0.00
## 15                       thal       0    0.00
## 16         has_heart_disease       0    0.00
```

The same reasoning applies when we want to remove (or keep) those variables above or below a certain threshold. Please check the missing values chapter to get more information about the implications when dealing with variables containing missing values.

1.1.1.4 Going deep into these topics

Values returned by `df_status` are deeply covered in other chapters:

- **Missing values** (NA) treatment, analysis, and imputation are deeply covered in the Missing Data chapter.
- **Data type**, its conversions and implications when handling different data types and more are covered in the Data Types chapter.
- A high number of **unique values** is synonymous for high-cardinality variables. This situation is studied in both

14

chapters:

- High Cardinality Variable in Descriptive Stats
- High Cardinality Variable in Predictive Modeling

1.1.1.5 Getting other common statistics: total rows, total columns and column names:

```
# Total rows
nrow(heart_disease)
```

```
## [1] 303
```

```
# Total columns
ncol(heart_disease)
```

```
## [1] 16
```

```
# Column names
colnames(heart_disease)
```

```
##  [1] "age"               "gender"
##  [3] "chest_pain"        "resting_blood_pressure"
##  [5] "serum_cholestoral" "fasting_blood_sugar"
##  [7] "resting_electro"   "max_heart_rate"
##  [9] "exer_angina"       "oldpeak"
## [11] "slope"             "num_vessels_flour"
## [13] "thal"              "heart_disease_severity"
## [15] "exter_angina"      "has_heart_disease"
```

1.1.2 Profiling categorical variables

Make sure you have the latest 'funModeling' version (>= 1.6).

Frequency or distribution analysis is made simple by the **freq** function. This retrieves the distribution in a table and a plot (by default) and shows the distribution of absolute and relative numbers.

If you want the distribution for two variables:

```
freq(data = heart_disease, input = c("thal",
  "chest_pain"))
```

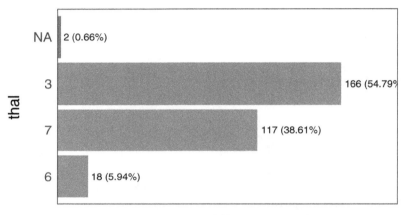

Figure 2: Frequency analysis 1

```
##     thal frequency percentage cumulative_perc
## 1      3       166      54.79           54.79
## 2      7       117      38.61           93.40
## 3      6        18       5.94           99.34
## 4  <NA>         2       0.66          100.00
```

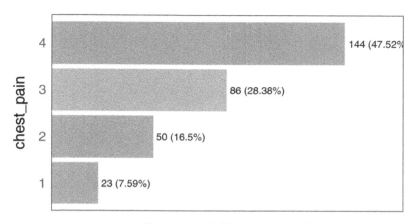

Frequency / (Percentage %)

Figure 3: Frequency analysis 2

```
##    chest_pain frequency percentage cumulative_perc
## 1           4       144      47.52           47.52
## 2           3        86      28.38           75.90
## 3           2        50      16.50           92.40
## 4           1        23       7.59          100.00
```

```
## [1] "Variables processed: thal, chest_pain"
```

As well as in the remaining **funModeling** functions, if input is missing, then it will run for all factor or character variables present in a given data frame:

```
freq(data = heart_disease)
```

If we only want to print the table excluding the plot, then we set the plot parameter to FALSE. The freq example can also handle a **single variable** as an input. By *default*, NA values **are considered** in both the table and the plot. If it is needed to exclude the NA then set na.rm = TRUE. Both examples in the following line:

```
freq(data = heart_disease$thal, plot = FALSE,
  na.rm = TRUE)
```

If only one variable is provided, then `freq` returns the printed table; thus, it is easy to perform some calculations based on the variables it provides.

- For example, to print the categories that represent most of the 80% of the share (based on `cumulative_perc` < 80).
- To get the categories belonging to the **long tail**, i.e., filtering by `percentage` < 1 by retrieving those categories appearing less than 1% of the time.

In addition, as with the other plot functions in the package, if there is a need to export plots, then add the **path_out** parameter, which will create the folder if it's not yet created.

```
freq(data = heart_disease, path_out = "my_folder")
```

1.1.2.0.1 Analysis

The output is ordered by the `frequency` variable, which quickly analyzes the most frequent categories and how many shares they represent (`cummulative_perc` variable). In general terms, we as human beings like order. If the variables are not ordered, then our eyes start moving over all the bars to do the comparison and our brains place each bar in relation to the other bars.

Check the difference for the same data input, first without order and then with order:

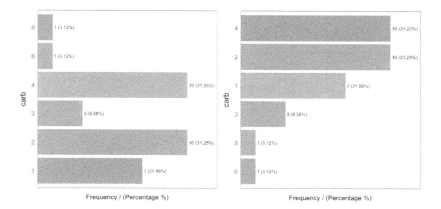

Figure 4: Order and beauty

Generally, there are just a few categories that appear most of the time.

A more complete analysis is in High Cardinality Variable in Descriptive Stats

1.1.2.1 Introducing the describe function

This function comes in the Hmisc package and allows us to quickly profile a complete dataset for both numerical and categorical variables. In this case, we'll select only two variables and we will analyze the result.

```
# Just keeping two variables to use in this example
heart_disease_3 = select(heart_disease, thal,
  chest_pain)

# Profiling the data!
describe(heart_disease_3)

## heart_disease_3
```

```
##
##   2  Variables        303  Observations
##   ----------------------------------------------------------
##  thal
##          n  missing  distinct
##        301        2        3
##
##  Value            3       6       7
##  Frequency      166      18     117
##  Proportion  0.551   0.060   0.389
##   ----------------------------------------------------------
##  chest_pain
##          n  missing  distinct
##        303        0        4
##
##  Value            1       2       3       4
##  Frequency       23      50      86     144
##  Proportion  0.076   0.165   0.284   0.475
##   ----------------------------------------------------------
```

Where:

- **n**: quantity of non-NA rows. In this case, it indicates there are 301 patients containing a number.
- **missing**: number of missing values. Summing this indicator to n gives us the total number of rows.
- **unique**: number of unique (or distinct) values.

The other information is pretty similar to the **freq** function and returns between parentheses the total number in relative and absolute values for each different category.

1.1.3   Profiling numerical variables

This section is separated into two parts:

- Part 1: Introducing the "World Data" case study
- Part 2: Doing the numerical profiling in R

If you don't want to know how the data preparation stage from Data World is calculated, then you can jump to "Part 2: Doing the numerical profiling in R", when the profiling started.

1.1.3.1   Part 1: Introducing the World Data case study

This contains many indicators regarding world development. Regardless the profiling example, the idea is to provide a ready-to-use table for sociologists, researchers, etc. interested in analyzing this kind of data.

The original data source is: http://databank.worldbank.org[17]. There you will find a data dictionary that explains all the variables.

First, we have to do some data wrangling. We are going to keep with the newest value per indicator.

```
library(Hmisc)
```

```
# Loading data from the book repository without altering
# the format
data_world = read.csv(file = "https://goo.gl/2TrDgN",
  header = T, stringsAsFactors = F, na.strings = "..")

# Excluding missing values in Series.Code. The data
# downloaded from the web page contains four lines with
# 'free-text' at the bottom of the file.
data_world = filter(data_world, Series.Code != "")
```

---

[17]http://databank.worldbank.org/data/reports.aspx?source=2&Topic=11#

```
# The magical function that keeps the newest values for
# each metric. If you're not familiar with R, then skip
# it.
max_ix <- function(d) {
  ix = which(!is.na(d))
  res = ifelse(length(ix) == 0, NA, d[max(ix)])
  return(res)
}


data_world$newest_value = apply(data_world[,
  5:ncol(data_world)], 1, FUN = max_ix)

# Printing the first three rows
head(data_world, 3)

##                                              Series.Name
## 1 Population living in slums (% of urban population)
## 2 Population living in slums (% of urban population)
## 3 Population living in slums (% of urban population)
##          Series.Code Country.Name Country.Code
## 1 EN.POP.SLUM.UR.ZS  Afghanistan           AFG
## 2 EN.POP.SLUM.UR.ZS      Albania           ALB
## 3 EN.POP.SLUM.UR.ZS      Algeria           DZA
##    X1990..YR1990. X2000..YR2000. X2007..YR2007.
## 1            NA             NA             NA
## 2            NA             NA             NA
## 3          11.8             NA             NA
##    X2008..YR2008. X2009..YR2009. X2010..YR2010.
## 1            NA             NA             NA
## 2            NA             NA             NA
## 3            NA             NA             NA
##    X2011..YR2011. X2012..YR2012. X2013..YR2013.
```

```
## 1              NA           NA           NA
## 2              NA           NA           NA
## 3              NA           NA           NA
##    X2014..YR2014. X2015..YR2015. X2016..YR2016.
## 1            62.7           NA           NA
## 2              NA           NA           NA
## 3              NA           NA           NA
##   newest_value
## 1         62.7
## 2           NA
## 3         11.8
```

The columns `Series.Name` and `Series.Code` are the indicators to be analyzed. `Country.Name` and `Country.Code` are the countries. Each row represents a unique combination of country and indicator. Remaining columns, `X1990..YR1990.` (year 1990),`X2000..YR2000.` (year 2000), `X2007..YR2007.` (year 2007), and so on indicate the metric value for that year, thus each column is a year.

1.1.3.2   Making a data scientist decision

There are many `NAs` because some countries don't have the measure of the indicator in those years. At this point, we need to **make a decision** as a data scientist. Probably no the optimal if we don't ask to an expert, e.g., a sociologist.

What to do with the `NA` values? In this case, we are going to to keep with the **newest value** for all the indicators. Perhaps this is not the best way to extract conclusions for a paper as we are going to compare some countries with information up to 2016 while other countries will be updated only to 2009. To compare all the indicators with the newest data is a valid approach for the first analysis.

Another solution could have been to keep with the newest value, but

23

only if this number belongs to the last five years. This would reduce the number of countries to analyze.

These questions are impossible to answer for an *artificial intelligence system*, yet the decision can change the results dramatically.

The last transformation

The next step will convert the last table from *long* to *wide* format. In other words, each row will represent a country and each column an indicator (thanks to the last transformation that has the *newest value* for each combination of indicator-country).

The indicator names are unclear, so we will "translate" a few of them.

```
# Get the list of indicator descriptions.
names=unique(select(data_world, Series.Name, Series.Code))
head(names, 5)
```

```
##                                             Series.Name
## 1     Population living in slums (% of urban population)
## 218                       Income share held by second 20%
## 435                        Income share held by third 20%
## 652                       Income share held by fourth 20%
## 869                      Income share held by highest 20%
##              Series.Code
## 1     EN.POP.SLUM.UR.ZS
## 218       SI.DST.02ND.20
## 435       SI.DST.03RD.20
## 652       SI.DST.04TH.20
## 869       SI.DST.05TH.20
```

```
# Convert a few
df_conv_world=data.frame(
  new_name=c("urban_poverty_headcount",
             "rural_poverty_headcount",
```

```
              "gini_index",
              "pop_living_slums",
              "poverty_headcount_1.9"),
   Series.Code=c("SI.POV.URHC",
                 "SI.POV.RUHC",
                 "SI.POV.GINI",
                 "EN.POP.SLUM.UR.ZS",
                 "SI.POV.DDAY"),
   stringsAsFactors = F)


# adding the new indicator value
data_world_2 = left_join(data_world,
                         df_conv_world,
                         by="Series.Code",
                         all.x=T)

data_world_2 =
   mutate(data_world_2, Series.Code_2=
          ifelse(!is.na(new_name),
                 as.character(data_world_2$new_name),
                 data_world_2$Series.Code)
          )
```

Any indicator meaning can be checked in data.worldbank.org. For example, if we want to know what EN.POP.SLUM.UR.ZS means, then we type: http://data.worldbank.org/indicator/EN.POP.SLUM.UR.ZS

```
# The package 'reshape2' contains both 'dcast' and 'melt'
# functions
library(reshape2)

data_world_wide = dcast(data_world_2, Country.Name ~
   Series.Code_2, value.var = "newest_value")
```

Note: To understand more about **long** and **wide** format using **reshape2** package, and how to convert from one to another, please go to http://seananderson.ca/2013/10/19/reshape.html.

Now we have the final table to analyze:

```
# Printing the first three rows
head(data_world_wide, 3)
```

```
##    Country.Name gini_index pop_living_slums
## 1  Afghanistan          NA             62.7
## 2       Albania      28.96               NA
## 3       Algeria          NA             11.8
##    poverty_headcount_1.9 rural_poverty_headcount
## 1                     NA                    38.3
## 2                   1.06                    15.3
## 3                     NA                     4.8
##    SI.DST.02ND.20 SI.DST.03RD.20 SI.DST.04TH.20
## 1              NA             NA             NA
## 2           13.17          17.34          22.81
## 3              NA             NA             NA
##    SI.DST.05TH.20 SI.DST.10TH.10 SI.DST.FRST.10
## 1              NA             NA             NA
## 2           37.82          22.93           3.66
## 3              NA             NA             NA
##    SI.DST.FRST.20 SI.POV.2DAY SI.POV.GAP2 SI.POV.GAPS
## 1              NA          NA          NA          NA
## 2            8.85        6.79        1.43        0.22
## 3              NA          NA          NA          NA
##    SI.POV.NAGP SI.POV.NAHC SI.POV.RUGP SI.POV.URGP
## 1          8.4        35.8         9.3         5.6
## 2          2.9        14.3         3.0         2.9
## 3           NA         5.5         0.8         1.1
##    SI.SPR.PC40 SI.SPR.PC40.ZG SI.SPR.PCAP SI.SPR.PCAP.ZG
```

```
## 1                 NA            NA          NA             NA
## 2              4.08       -1.2205        7.41        -1.3143
## 3                 NA            NA          NA             NA
##    urban_poverty_headcount
## 1                     27.6
## 2                     13.6
## 3                      5.8
```

1.1.3.3 Part 2: Doing the numerical profiling in R

We will see the following functions:

- describe from Hmisc
- profiling_num (full univariate analysis), and plot_num (hisotgrams) from funModeling

We'll pick up only two variables as an example:

```
library(Hmisc)  # contains the `describe` function

vars_to_profile = c("gini_index",
  "poverty_headcount_1.9")
data_subset = select(data_world_wide,
  one_of(vars_to_profile))

# Using the `describe` on a complete dataset. # It can be
# run with one variable; for example,
# describe(data_subset$poverty_headcount_1.9)

describe(data_subset)

## data_subset
##
##  2  Variables      217  Observations
## -----------------------------------------------------------
```

```
## gini_index
##           n  missing distinct      Info      Mean       Gmd
##         140       77      136         1      38.8     9.594
##         .05      .10      .25       .50       .75       .90
##       26.81    27.58    32.35     37.69     43.92     50.47
##         .95
##       53.53
##
## lowest : 24.09 25.59 25.90 26.12 26.13
## highest: 56.24 60.46 60.79 60.97 63.38
## ------------------------------------------------------------
## poverty_headcount_1.9
##           n  missing distinct      Info      Mean       Gmd
##         116      101      107         1     18.33     23.56
##         .05      .10      .25       .50       .75       .90
##       0.025    0.075    1.052     6.000    33.815    54.045
##         .95
##      67.328
##
## lowest :  0.00  0.01  0.03  0.04  0.06
## highest: 68.64 68.74 70.91 77.08 77.84
## ------------------------------------------------------------
```

Taking `poverty_headcount_1.9` (*Poverty headcount ratio at $1.90 a day is the percentage of the population living on less than $1.90 a day at 2011 international prices.*), we can describe it as:

- **n**: quantity of non-NA rows. In this case, it indicates 116 countries that contain a number.
- **missing**: number of missing values. Summing this indicator to n gives us the total number of rows. Almost half of the countries have no data.
- **unique**: number of unique (or distinct) values.
- **Info**: an estimator of the amount of information present in the

variable and not important at this point.

- **Mean**: the classical mean or average.
- Numbers: .05, .10, .25, .50, .75, .90 and .95 stand for the percentiles. These values are really useful since it helps us to describe the distribution. It will be deeply covered later on, i.e., .05 is the 5th percentile.
- **lowest** and **highest**: the five lowest/highest values. Here, we can spot outliers and data errors. For example, if the variable represents a percentage, then it cannot contain negative values.

The next function is `profiling_num` which takes a data frame and retrieves a *big* table, easy to get overwhelmed in a *sea of metrics*. This is similar to what we can see in the movie *The Matrix*.

Figure 5: The matrix of data

Picture from the movie: "The Matrix" (1999). The Wachowski Brothers (Directors).

The idea of the following table is to give to the user a **full set of metrics,**, for then, she or he can decide which ones to pick for the study.

Note: Every metric has a lot of statistical theory behind it. Here we'll be covering just a tiny and **oversimplified** approach to introduce the concepts.

```
library(funModeling)

# Full numerical profiling in one function automatically
# excludes non-numerical variables
profiling_num(data_world_wide)
```

```
##                          variable mean std_dev variation_coef
## 1                      gini_index 38.8    8.49           0.22
## 2                 pop_living_slums 45.7   23.66           0.52
## 3              poverty_headcount_1.9 18.3  22.74           1.24
## 4       rural_poverty_headcount 41.2   21.91           0.53
## 5                 SI.DST.02ND.20 10.9    2.17           0.20
## 6                 SI.DST.03RD.20 15.2    2.03           0.13
## 7                 SI.DST.04TH.20 21.5    1.49           0.07
## 8                 SI.DST.05TH.20 45.9    7.14           0.16
## 9                 SI.DST.10TH.10 30.5    6.75           0.22
## 10                SI.DST.FRST.10  2.5    0.87           0.34
## 11                SI.DST.FRST.20  6.5    1.87           0.29
## 12                   SI.POV.2DAY 32.4   30.64           0.95
## 13                   SI.POV.GAP2 14.2   16.40           1.16
## 14                   SI.POV.GAPS  6.9   10.10           1.46
## 15                   SI.POV.NAGP 12.2   10.12           0.83
## 16                   SI.POV.NAHC 30.7   17.88           0.58
## 17                   SI.POV.RUGP 15.9   11.83           0.75
## 18                   SI.POV.URGP  8.3    8.24           0.99
## 19                   SI.SPR.PC40 10.3    9.75           0.95
## 20                SI.SPR.PC40.ZG  2.0    3.62           1.85
## 21                   SI.SPR.PCAP 21.1   17.44           0.83
## 22                SI.SPR.PCAP.ZG  1.5    3.21           2.20
## 23 urban_poverty_headcount 23.3   15.06           0.65
##        p_01   p_05    p_25 p_50 p_75 p_95 p_99 skewness
## 1  25.711 26.815 32.348 37.7 43.9 53.5 60.9    0.552
## 2   6.830 10.750 25.175 46.2 65.6 83.4 93.4    0.087
```

```
## 3    0.000  0.025  1.052  6.0 33.8 67.3 76.2     1.125
## 4    2.902  6.465 25.250 38.1 57.6 75.8 81.7     0.051
## 5    5.568  7.361  9.527 11.1 12.6 14.2 14.6    -0.411
## 6    9.137 11.828 13.877 15.5 16.7 17.9 18.1    -0.876
## 7   16.286 18.288 20.758 21.9 22.5 23.0 23.4    -1.537
## 8   35.004 36.360 40.495 44.8 49.8 58.1 65.9     0.738
## 9   20.729 21.988 25.710 29.5 34.1 42.2 50.6     0.905
## 10   0.916  1.147  1.885  2.5  3.2  3.9  4.3     0.043
## 11   2.614  3.369  5.092  6.5  8.0  9.4 10.0    -0.119
## 12   0.061  0.393  3.828 20.3 63.2 84.6 90.3     0.536
## 13   0.012  0.085  1.305  5.5 26.3 48.5 56.2     1.063
## 14   0.000  0.000  0.287  1.4 10.3 31.5 38.3     1.654
## 15   0.421  1.225  4.500  8.7 16.9 32.4 36.7     1.129
## 16   1.842  6.430 16.350 26.6 44.2 63.0 71.6     0.529
## 17   0.740  1.650  5.950 13.6 22.5 37.7 45.3     0.801
## 18   0.300  0.900  2.900  6.3  9.9 25.1 35.2     2.316
## 19   0.857  1.228  3.475  6.9 12.7 28.9 35.4     1.251
## 20  -6.232 -3.021 -0.084  1.7  4.6  7.9  9.0    -0.294
## 21   2.426  3.138  8.003 15.3 25.4 52.8 67.2     1.132
## 22  -5.897 -3.805 -0.486  1.3  3.6  7.0  8.5    -0.018
## 23   0.579  3.140 12.708 20.1 31.2 51.0 61.8     0.730
##     kurtosis  iqr      range_98       range_80
## 1        2.9 11.6  [25.71, 60.9] [27.58, 50.47]
## 2        2.0 40.5  [6.83, 93.41]   [12.5, 75.2]
## 3        2.9 32.8    [0, 76.15]  [0.08, 54.05]
## 4        2.0 32.3   [2.9, 81.7] [13.99, 71.99]
## 5        2.7  3.1 [5.57, 14.57]   [8.28, 13.8]
## 6        3.8  2.8 [9.14, 18.14]  [12.67, 17.5]
## 7        5.6  1.8 [16.29, 23.39] [19.73, 22.81]
## 8        3.3  9.3   [35, 65.89] [36.99, 55.24]
## 9        3.6  8.4 [20.73, 50.62] [22.57, 39.89]
## 10       2.2  1.4  [0.92, 4.35]   [1.48, 3.67]
## 11       2.2  2.9   [2.61, 10]   [3.99, 8.89]
```

```
## 12       1.8 59.4   [0.06, 90.34]   [0.79, 78.29]
## 13       2.9 25.0   [0.01, 56.18]   [0.16, 40.85]
## 14       4.7 10.0      [0, 38.29]   [0.02, 23.45]
## 15       4.0 12.4   [0.42, 36.72]      [1.85, 27]
## 16       2.4 27.9   [1.84, 71.64]   [9.86, 58.22]
## 17       3.0 16.5   [0.74, 45.29]     [3.3, 32.2]
## 18       9.8  7.0    [0.3, 35.17]     [1.3, 19.1]
## 19       3.4  9.2   [0.86, 35.35]   [1.81, 27.63]
## 20       3.3  4.7      [-6.23, 9]   [-2.64, 6.48]
## 21       3.3 17.4   [2.43, 67.17]   [4.25, 49.22]
## 22       3.6  4.0    [-5.9, 8.48]   [-2.07, 5.17]
## 23       3.0 18.5   [0.58, 61.75]   [5.98, 46.11]
```

Each indicator has *its raison d'être*:

- `variable`: variable name

- `mean`: the well-known mean or average

- `std_dev`: standard deviation, a measure of **dispersion** or **spread** around the mean value. A value around 0 means almost no variation (thus, it seems more like a constant); on the other side, it is harder to set what *high* is, but we can tell that the higher the variation the greater the spread. *Chaos may look like infinite standard variation*. The unit is the same as the mean so that it can be compared.

- `variation_coef`: variation coefficient=std_dev/mean. Because the `std_dev` is an absolute number, it's good to have an indicator that puts it in a relative number, comparing the `std_dev` against the `mean` A value of 0.22 indicates the `std_dev` is 22% of the `mean` If it were close to 0 then the variable tends to be more centered around the mean. If we compare two classifiers, then we may prefer the one with less `std_dev` and `variation_coef` on its accuracy.

- p_01, p_05, p_25, p_50, p_75, p_95, p_99: **Percentiles** at 1%, 5%, 25%, and so on. Later on in this chapter is a complete review about percentiles.

For a full explanation about percentiles, please go to: Annex 1: The magic of percentiles.

- skewness: is a measure of *asymmetry*. Close to **0** indicates that the distribution is *equally* distributed (or symmetrical) around its mean. A **positive number** implies a long tail on the right, whereas a **negative number** means the opposite. After this section, check the skewness in the plots. The variable pop_living_slums is close to 0 ("equally" distributed), poverty_headcount_1.9 is positive (tail on the right), and SI.DST.04TH.20 is negative (tail on the left). The further the skewness is from 0 the more likely the distribution is to have **outliers**

- kurtosis: describes the distribution **tails**; keeping it simple, a higher number may indicate the presence of outliers (just as we'll see later for the variable SI.POV.URGP holding an outlier around the value 50 For a complete skewness and kurtosis review, check Refs. (McNeese 2016) and (Handbook 2013).

- iqr: the inter-quartile range is the result of looking at percentiles 0.25 and 0.75 and indicates, in the same variable unit, the dispersion length of 50% of the values. The higher the value the more sparse the variable.

- range_98 and range_80: indicates the range where 98% of the values are. It removes the bottom and top 1% (thus, the 98% number). It is good to know the variable range without potential outliers. For example, pop_living_slums goes from 0 to 76.15 It's **more robust** than comparing the **min** and **max** values. The range_80 is the same as the **range_98** but without the bottom

33

and top 10%

iqr, `range_98` and `range_80` are based on percentiles, which we'll be covering later in this chapter.

Important: All the metrics are calculated having removed the `NA` values. Otherwise, the table would be filled with NA's.

1.1.3.3.1 Advice when using `profiling_num`

The idea of `profiling_num` is to provide to the data scientist with a full set of metrics, so they can select the most relevant. This can easily be done using the `select` function from the `dplyr` package.

In addition, we have to set in `profiling_num` the parameter `print_results = FALSE`. This way we avoid the printing in the console.

For example, let's get with the **mean, p_01, p_99** and **range_80**:

```
my_profiling_table = profiling_num(data_world_wide,
    print_results = FALSE) %>% select(variable, mean,
    p_01, p_99, range_80)

# Printing only the first three rows
head(my_profiling_table, 3)
```

```
##                     variable mean p_01 p_99       range_80
## 1                 gini_index   39 25.7   61 [27.58, 50.47]
## 2           pop_living_slums   46  6.8   93   [12.5, 75.2]
## 3 poverty_headcount_1.9        18  0.0   76  [0.08, 54.05]
```

Please note that `profiling_num` returns a table, so we can quickly filter cases given on the conditions we set.

1.1.3.3.2 Profiling numerical variables by plotting

34

Another function in `funModeling` is `plot_num` which takes a dataset and plots the distribution of every numerical variable while automatically excluding the non-numerical ones:

`plot_num(data_world_wide)`

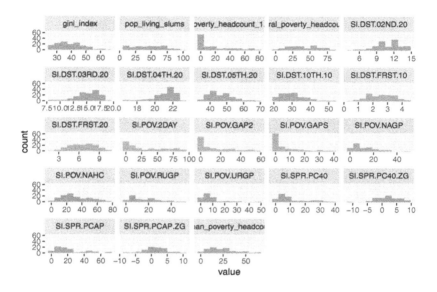

Figure 6: Profiling numerical data

We can adjust the number of bars used in the plot by changing the `bins` parameter (default value is set to 10). For example: `plot_num(data_world_wide, bins = 20)`.

1.1.4 Final thoughts

Many numbers have appeared here so far, *and even more in the percentile appendix*. The important point is for you to find the right approach to explore your data. This can come from other metrics or other criteria.

The functions `df_status`, `describe`, `freq`, `profiling_num` and `plot_num` can be run at the beginning of a data project.

Regarding the **normal and abnormal behavior** on data, it's important to study both. To describe the dataset in general terms, we should exclude the extreme values: for example, with `range_98` variable. The mean should decrease after the exclusion.

These analyses are **univariate**; that is, they do not take into account other variables (**multivariate** analysis). This will be part of this book later on. Meanwhile, for the correlation between input (and output) variables, you can check the Correlation chapter.

Data Science Live Book

1.2 Correlation and Relationship

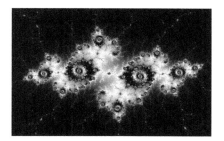

Manderbolt fractal, where the chaos expresses its beauty; image source: Wikipedia.

1.2.1 What is this about?

This chapter contains both methodological and practical aspects of measuring correlation in variables. We will see that *correlation* word can be translated into "**functional relationship**".

In methodological you will find the Anscombe Quartet, a set of four plots with dissimilar spatial distribution, but sharing the same correlation measure. We'll go one step ahead re-calculating their relationship though a more robust metric (MIC).

We will mention **Information Theory** several times, although by now it's not going to be covered at the mathematical level, it's planned to. Many algorithms are based on it, even deep learning.

Understanding these concepts in low dimension (two variables) and small data (a bunch of rows) allow us to better understand high dimensional data. Nonetheless, some real cases are only *small* data.

From the practical point of view, you'll be able to replicate the analysis with your own data, profiling and exposing their relationships in fancy plots.

Let's starting loading all needed libraries.

```r
# Loading needed libraries
library(funModeling)  # contains heart_disease data
library(minerva)  # contains MIC statistic
library(ggplot2)
library(dplyr)
library(reshape2)
library(gridExtra)  # allow us to plot two plots in a row
options(scipen = 999)  # disable scientific notation
```

1.2.2 Linear correlation

Perhaps the most standard correlation measure for numeric variables is the R statistic (or Pearson coefficient) which goes from 1 *positive correlation* to -1 *negative correlation*. A value around 0 implies no correlation.

Consider the following example, which calculates R measure based on a target variable (for example to do feature engineering). Function correlation_table retrieves R metric for all numeric variables skipping the categorical/nominal ones.

```r
correlation_table(data = heart_disease,
  target = "has_heart_disease")
```

```
##                       Variable has_heart_disease
## 1        has_heart_disease                  1.00
## 2 heart_disease_severity                  0.83
## 3        num_vessels_flour                  0.46
## 4                  oldpeak                  0.42
## 5                    slope                  0.34
## 6                      age                  0.23
```

```
## 7 resting_blood_pressure          0.15
## 8        serum_cholestoral         0.08
## 9          max_heart_rate         -0.42
```

Variable `heart_disease_severity` is the most important -numerical-variable, the higher its value the higher the chances of having a heart disease (positive correlation). Just the opposite to `max_heart_rate`, which has a negative correlation.

Squaring this number returns the `R-squared` statistic (aka R2), which goes from 0 *no correlation* to 1 *high correlation*.

R statistic is highly influenced by **outliers** and **non-linear** relationships.

1.2.2.1   Correlation on Anscombe's Quartet

Take a look at the **Anscombe's quartet**, quoting Wikipedia[18]:

> They were constructed in 1973 by the statistician Francis Anscombe to demonstrate both the importance of graphing data before analyzing it and the effect of outliers on statistical properties.

1973 and still valid, fantastic.

These four relationships are different, but all of them have the same R2: `0.816`.

Following example calculates the R2 and plot every pair.

```
# Reading anscombe quartet data
anscombe_data =
  read.delim(file="https://goo.gl/mVLz5L", header = T)

# calculating the correlation (R squared, or R2) for
```

---

[18]https://en.wikipedia.org/wiki/Anscombe%27s_quartet

```r
#every pair, every value is the same: 0.86.
cor_1 = cor(anscombe_data$x1, anscombe_data$y1)
cor_2 = cor(anscombe_data$x2, anscombe_data$y2)
cor_3 = cor(anscombe_data$x3, anscombe_data$y3)
cor_4 = cor(anscombe_data$x4, anscombe_data$y4)


# defining the function
plot_anscombe <- function(x, y, value, type)
{
  # 'anscombe_data' is a global variable, this is
  # a bad programming practice ;)
  p=ggplot(anscombe_data, aes_string(x,y))  +
    geom_smooth(method='lm', fill=NA) +
    geom_point(aes(colour=factor(1),
                   fill = factor(1)),
               shape=21, size = 2
               ) +
    ylim(2, 13) +
    xlim(4, 19) +
    theme_minimal() +
    theme(legend.position="none") +
    annotate("text",
             x = 12,
             y =4.5,
             label =
               sprintf("%s: %s",
                       type,
                       round(value,2)
                       )
             )

  return(p)
```

```
}
```

```
# plotting in a 2x2 grid
grid.arrange(plot_anscombe("x1", "y1", cor_1, "R2"),
             plot_anscombe("x2", "y2", cor_2, "R2"),
             plot_anscombe("x3", "y3", cor_3, "R2"),
             plot_anscombe("x4", "y4", cor_4, "R2"),
             ncol=2,
             nrow=2)
```

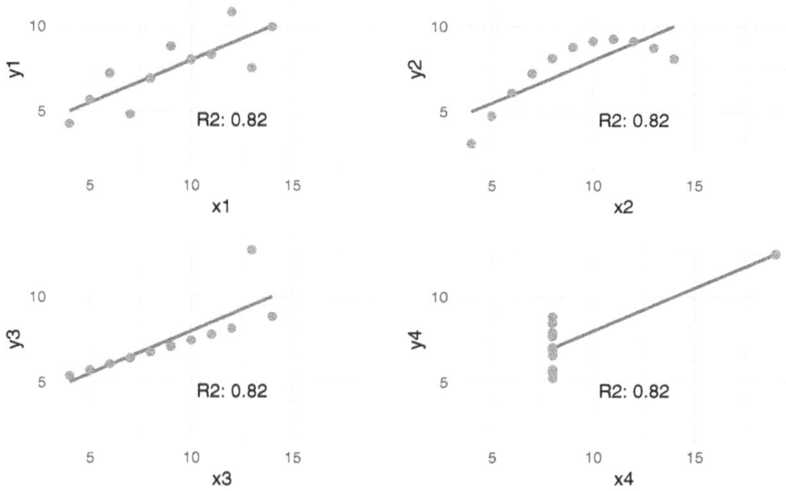

Figure 7: Anscombe set

4-different plots, having the same **mean** for every **x** and **y** variable (9 and 7.501 respectively), and the same degree of correlation. You can check all the measures by typing **summary(anscombe_data)**.

This is why is so important to plot relationships when analyzing correlations.

We'll back on this data later. It can be improved! First, we'll introduce some concepts of information theory.

1.2.3 Correlation based on Information Theory

This relationships can be measure better with Information Theory[19] concepts. One of the many algorithms to measure correlation based on this is: **MINE**, acronym for: Maximal Information-based nonparametric exploration.

The implementation in R can be found in minerva[20] package. It's also available in other languages like Python.

1.2.3.1 An example in R: A perfect relationship

Let's plot a non-linear relationship, directly based on a function (negative exponential), and print the MIC value.

```
x = seq(0, 20, length.out = 500)
df_exp = data.frame(x = x, y = dexp(x, rate = 0.65))
ggplot(df_exp, aes(x = x, y = y)) +
  geom_line(color = "steelblue") +
  theme_minimal()
```

---

[19]https://en.wikipedia.org/wiki/Information_theory
[20]https://cran.r-project.org/web/packages/minerva/index.html

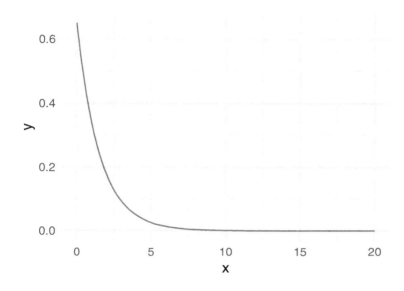

Figure 8: A perfect relationship

```
# position [1,2] contains the correlation of both
# variables, excluding the correlation measure of each
# variable against itself.

# Calculating linear correlation
res_cor_R2 = cor(df_exp)[1, 2]^2
sprintf("R2: %s", round(res_cor_R2, 2))

## [1] "R2: 0.39"

# now computing the MIC metric
res_mine = mine(df_exp)
sprintf("MIC: %s", res_mine$MIC[1, 2])

## [1] "MIC: 1"
```

MIC value goes from 0 to 1. Being 0 implies no correlation and 1 highest correlation. The interpretation is the same as the R-squared.

1.2.3.2   Results analysis

The `MIC=1` indicates there is a perfect correlation between the two variables. If we were doing **feature engineering** this variable should be included.

Further than a simple correlation, what the MIC says is: "Hey these two variables show a functional relationship".

In machine learning terms (and oversimplifying): "variable y is dependant of variable x and a function -that we don't know which one- can be found model the relationship."

This is tricky because that relationship was effectively created based on a function, an exponential one.

But let's continue with other examples...

1.2.4   Adding noise

Noise is an undesired signal adding to the original one. In machine learning noise helps the model to get confused. Concretely: two identical input cases -for example customers- have different outcomes -one buy and the other doesn't-.

Now we are going to add some noise creating the `y_noise_1` variable.

```
df_exp$y_noise_1 = jitter(df_exp$y, factor = 1000,
  amount = NULL)
ggplot(df_exp, aes(x = x, y = y_noise_1)) +
  geom_line(color = "steelblue") + theme_minimal()
```

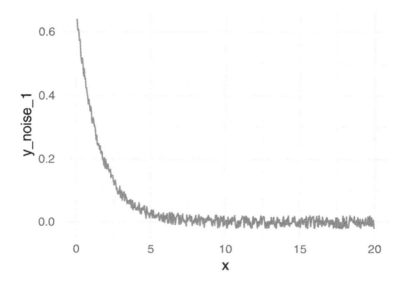

Figure 9: Adding some noise

Calculating the correlation and MIC again, printing in both cases the entire matrix, which shows the correlation/MIC metric of each input variable against all the others including themselves.

```
# calculating R squared
res_R2 = cor(df_exp)^2
res_R2
```

```
##                x    y y_noise_1
## x           1.00 0.39      0.39
## y           0.39 1.00      0.99
## y_noise_1   0.39 0.99      1.00
```

```
# Calculating mine
res_mine_2 = mine(df_exp)
```

```
# Printing MIC
res_mine_2$MIC
```

```
##              x    y y_noise_1
## x         1.00 1.00      0.74
## y         1.00 1.00      0.73
## y_noise_1 0.74 0.73      1.00
```

Adding noise to the data decreases the MIC value from 1 to 0.7226365 (-27%), and this is great!

R2 also decreased but just a little bit, from 0.3899148 to 0.3866319 (-0.8%).

Conclusion: MIC reflects a noisy relationship much better than R2, and it's helpful to find correlated associations.

About the last example: Generate data based on a function is only for teaching purposes. But the concept of noise in variables is quite common in *almost* **every data set**, no matter its source. You don't have to do anything to add noise to variables, it's already there. Machine learning models deal with this noise, by approaching to the *real* shape of data.

It's quite useful to use the MIC measure to get a sense of the information present in a relationship between two variables.

1.2.5   Measuring non-linearity (MIC-R2)

`mine` function returns several metrics, we checked only **MIC**, but due to the nature of the algorithm (you can check the original paper (Reshef et al. 2011)), it computes more interesting indicators. Check them all by inspecting `res_mine_2` object.

46

One of them is `MICR2`, used as a measure of **non-linearity**. It is calculated by doing the: MIC - R2. Since R2 measures the linearity, a high `MICR2` would indicate a non-linear relationship.

We can check it by calculating the MICR2 manually, following two matrix returns the same result:

```
# MIC r2: non-linearity metric
round(res_mine_2$MICR2, 3)
# calculating MIC r2 manually
round(res_mine_2$MIC - res_R2, 3)
```

Non-linear relationships are harder to build a model, even more using a linear algorithm like decision trees or linear regression.

Imagine we need to explain the relationship to another person, we'll need "more words" to do it. It's easier to say: *"A increases as B increases and the ratio is always 3x"* (if A=1 then B=3, linear).

In comparison to: *"A increases as B increases, but A is almost 0 until B reaches the value 10, then A raises to 300; and when B reaches 15, A goes to 1000."*

```
# creating data example
df_example=data.frame(x=df_exp$x,
                      y_exp=df_exp$y,
                      y_linear=3*df_exp$x+2)


# getting mine metrics
res_mine_3=mine(df_example)


# generating labels to print the results
results_linear =
  sprintf("MIC: %s \n MIC-R2 (non-linearity): %s",
          res_mine_3$MIC[1,3],
          round(res_mine_3$MICR2[1,3],2)
```

```
        )

results_exp =
  sprintf("MIC: %s \n MIC-R2 (non-linearity): %s",
          res_mine_3$MIC[1,2],
          round(res_mine_3$MICR2[1,2],4)
          )

# Plotting results
# Creating plot exponential variable
p_exp=ggplot(df_example, aes(x=x, y=y_exp)) +
  geom_line(color='steelblue') +
  annotate("text", x = 11, y =0.4, label = results_exp) +
  theme_minimal()

# Creating plot linear variable
p_linear=ggplot(df_example, aes(x=x, y=y_linear)) +
  geom_line(color='steelblue') +
  annotate("text", x = 8, y = 55,
           label = results_linear) +
  theme_minimal()

grid.arrange(p_exp,p_linear,ncol=2)
```

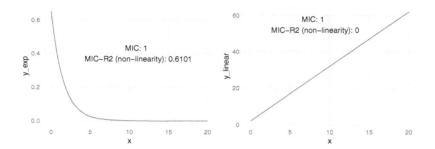

Figure 10: Comparing relationships

Both plots show a perfect correlation (or relationship), holding an MIC=1. Regarding non-linearity, MICR2 behaves as expected, in y_exp=0.6101, and in y_linear=0.

This point is important since the **MIC behaves like R2 does in linear relationships**, plus it adapts quite well to **non-linear** relationships as we saw before, retrieving a particular score metric (MICR2) to profile the relationship.

1.2.6   Measuring information on Anscombe Quartet

Remember the example we review at the beginning? Every pair of Anscombe Quartet returns a **R2 of 0.86**. But based on its plots it was clearly that not every pair exhibits neither a good correlation nor a similar distribution of x and y.

But what happen if we measure the relationship with a metric based on Information Theory? Yes, MIC again.

```
# calculating the MIC for every pair
mic_1 = mine(anscombe_data$x1, anscombe_data$y1,
  alpha = 0.8)$MIC
```

```
mic_2 = mine(anscombe_data$x2, anscombe_data$y2,
   alpha = 0.8)$MIC
mic_3 = mine(anscombe_data$x3, anscombe_data$y3,
   alpha = 0.8)$MIC
mic_4 = mine(anscombe_data$x4, anscombe_data$y4,
   alpha = 0.8)$MIC

# plotting MIC in a 2x2 grid
grid.arrange(plot_anscombe("x1", "y1", mic_1,
   "MIC"), plot_anscombe("x2", "y2", mic_2,
   "MIC"), plot_anscombe("x3", "y3", mic_3,
   "MIC"), plot_anscombe("x4", "y4", mic_4,
   "MIC"), ncol = 2, nrow = 2)
```

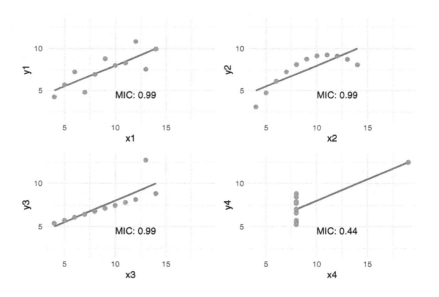

Figure 11: MIC statistic

As you may notice we increased the **alpha** value to 0.8, this is a good practice -according to the documentation- when we analyzed small samples. The default value is 0.6 and its maximum 1.

In this case, MIC value spotted the most spurious relationship in the pair x4 - y4. Probably due to a few cases per plot (11 rows) the MIC was the same for all the others pairs. Having more cases will show different MIC values.

But when combining the MIC with **MIC-R2** (non-linearity measurement) new insights appears:

```
# Calculating the MIC for every pair, note the 'MIC-R2'
# object has the hyphen when the input are two vectors,
# unlike when it takes a data frame which is 'MICR2'.
mic_r2_1 = mine(anscombe_data$x1, anscombe_data$y1,
  alpha = 0.8)$`MIC-R2`
mic_r2_2 = mine(anscombe_data$x2, anscombe_data$y2,
  alpha = 0.8)$`MIC-R2`
mic_r2_3 = mine(anscombe_data$x3, anscombe_data$y3,
  alpha = 0.8)$`MIC-R2`
mic_r2_4 = mine(anscombe_data$x4, anscombe_data$y4,
  alpha = 0.8)$`MIC-R2`


# Ordering according mic_r2
df_mic_r2 = data.frame(pair = c(1, 2, 3, 4),
  mic_r2 = c(mic_r2_1, mic_r2_2, mic_r2_3,
    mic_r2_4)) %>% arrange(-mic_r2)
df_mic_r2


##    pair mic_r2
## 1     2   0.33
## 2     3   0.33
## 3     1   0.33
## 4     4  -0.23
```

Ordering decreasingly by its **non-linearity** the results are consisent with the plots: $2 > 3 > 1 > 4$. Something strange for pair 4, a negative number. This is because MIC is lower than the R2. A relationship that worth to be plotted.

1.2.7 Measuring non-monotonicity: MAS measure

MINE can also help us to profile time series regarding its non-monotonicity with **MAS** (maximum asymmetry score).

A monotonic series is such it never changes its tendency, it always goes up or down. More on this on (Wikipedia 2017b).

Following example simulates two-time series, one not-monotonic `y_1` and the other monotonic `y_2`.

```
# creating sample data (simulating time series)
time_x=sort(runif(n=1000, min=0, max=1))
y_1=4*(time_x-0.5)^2
y_2=4*(time_x-0.5)^3

# Calculating MAS for both series
mas_y1=round(mine(time_x,y_1)$MAS,2)
mas_y2=mine(time_x,y_2)$MAS

# Putting all together
df_mono=data.frame(time_x=time_x, y_1=y_1, y_2=y_2)

# Plotting
label_p_y_1 =
  sprintf("MAS=%s (goes down \n and up => not-monotonic)",
          mas_y1)

p_y_1=ggplot(df_mono, aes(x=time_x, y=y_1)) +
```

```
geom_line(color='steelblue') +
theme_minimal()   +
annotate("text", x = 0.45, y =0.75,
         label = label_p_y_1)

label_p_y_2=
  sprintf("MAS=%s (goes up => monotonic)", mas_y2)

p_y_2=ggplot(df_mono, aes(x=time_x, y=y_2)) +
  geom_line(color='steelblue') +
  theme_minimal() +
  annotate("text", x = 0.43, y =0.35,
           label = label_p_y_2)

grid.arrange(p_y_1,p_y_2,ncol=2)
```

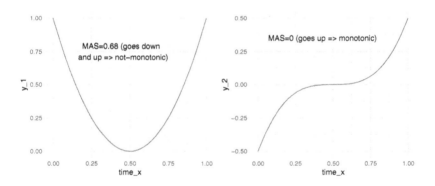

Figure 12: Monotonicity in functions

From another perspective, MAS is also useful to detect periodic relationships. Let's illustrate this with an example

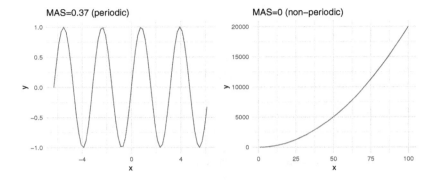

Figure 13: Periodicity in functions

1.2.7.1 A more real example: Time Series

Consider the following case which contains three-time series: **y1**, **y2**
and **y3**. They can be profiled concerning its non-monotonicity or overall
growth trend.

```
# reading data
df_time_series =
  read.delim(file="https://goo.gl/QDUjfd")


# converting to long format so they can be plotted
df_time_series_long=melt(df_time_series, id="time")

# Plotting
plot_time_series =
  ggplot(data=df_time_series_long,
         aes(x=time, y=value, colour=variable)) +
  geom_line() +
  theme_minimal() +
  scale_color_brewer(palette="Set2")
```

```
plot_time_series
```

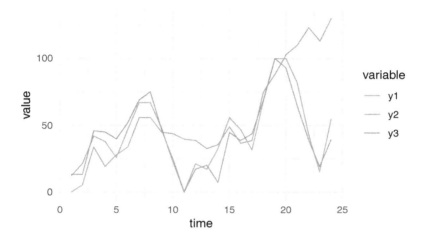

Figure 14: Time series example

```
# Calculating and printing MAS values for time series
# data
mine_ts = mine(df_time_series)
mine_ts$MAS
```

```
##         time     y1     y2     y3
## time 0.00 0.120 0.105 0.191
## y1   0.12 0.000 0.068 0.081
## y2   0.11 0.068 0.000 0.057
## y3   0.19 0.081 0.057 0.000
```

We need to look at `time` column, so we've got the MAS value of each series regarding the time. `y2` is the most monotonic (and less periodic) series, and it can be confirmed by looking at it. It seems to be always up.

MAS summary:

- MAS ~ 0 indicates monotonic or non-periodic function ("always" up or down)
- MAS ~ 1 indicates non-monotonic or periodic function

1.2.8   Correlation between time series

MIC metric can also measure the **correlation in time series**, it is not a general purpose tool but can be helpful to compare different series quickly.

This section is based on the same data we used in MAS example.

```
# printing again the 3-time series
plot_time_series
```

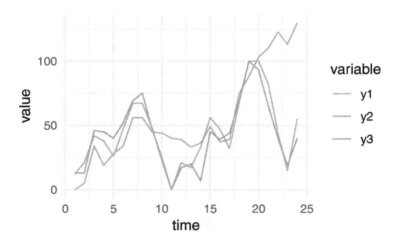

Figure 15: Time series example

56

```
# Printing MIC values
mine_ts$MIC
```

```
##         time   y1   y2   y3
## time 1.00 0.38 0.69 0.34
## y1    0.38 1.00 0.62 0.71
## y2    0.69 0.62 1.00 0.52
## y3    0.34 0.71 0.52 1.00
```

Now we need to look at y1 column. According to MIC measure, we can confirm the same that it's shown in last plot:

y1 is more similar to y3 (MIC=0.709) than what is y2 (MIC=0.61).

1.2.8.1 Going further: Dynamic Time Warping

MIC will not be helpful for more complex esenarios having time series which vary in speed, you would use dynamic time warping[21] technique (**DTW**).

Let's use an image to catch up the concept visually:

---

[21] https://en.wikipedia.org/wiki/Dynamic_time_warping

Based on euclidean distance

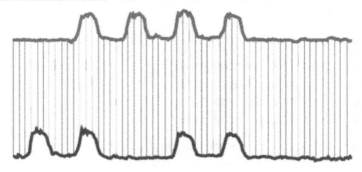

Based on Dynamic Time Wrapping

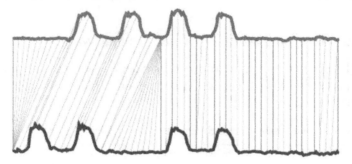

Figure 16: Dynamic time warping

Image source: *Dynamic time wrapping Converting images into time series for data mining* (Izbicki 2011).

The last image shows two different approaches to compare time series, and the **euclidean** is more similar to MIC measure. While DTW can track similarities occurring at different times.

A nice implementation in **R**: dtw package[22].

---

[22]http://dtw.r-forge.r-project.org

Finding correlations between time series is another way of performing **time series clustering**.

1.2.9 Correlation on categorical variables

MINE -and many other algorithms- only work with numerical data. We need to do a **data preparation** trick, converting every categorical variable into flag (or dummy variable).

If the original categorical variable has 30 possible values, it will result in 30 new columns holding the value 0 or 1, when 1 represents the presence of that category in the row.

If we use package `caret` from R, this conversion only takes two lines of code:

```
library(caret)

# selecting just a few variables
heart_disease_2 =
  select(heart_disease, max_heart_rate, oldpeak,
         thal, chest_pain,exer_angina, has_heart_disease)

# this conversion from categorical to a numeric is merely
# to have a cleaner plot
heart_disease_2$has_heart_disease=
  ifelse(heart_disease_2$has_heart_disease=="yes", 1, 0)

# it converts all categorical variables (factor and
# character for R) into numerical variables.
# skipping the original so the data is ready to use
dmy = dummyVars(" ~ .", data = heart_disease_2)

heart_disease_3 =
```

```
data.frame(predict(dmy, newdata = heart_disease_2))

# Important: If you recieve this message
# `Error: Missing values present in input variable 'x'.
# Consider using use = 'pairwise.complete.obs'.`
# is because data has missing values.
# Please don't omit NA without an impact analysis first,
# in this case it is not important.
heart_disease_4=na.omit(heart_disease_3)

# compute the mic!
mine_res_hd=mine(heart_disease_4)
```

Printing a sample. . .

```
mine_res_hd$MIC[1:5, 1:5]
```

```
##                    max_heart_rate oldpeak thal.3 thal.6
## max_heart_rate               1.00    0.24  0.244  0.120
## oldpeak                      0.24    1.00  0.175  0.111
## thal.3                       0.24    0.18  0.992  0.073
## thal.6                       0.12    0.11  0.073  0.327
## thal.7                       0.18    0.16  0.710  0.044
##                    thal.7
## max_heart_rate      0.184
## oldpeak             0.157
## thal.3              0.710
## thal.6              0.044
## thal.7              0.964
```

Where column thal.3 takes a value of 1 when thal=3.

1.2.9.1 Printing some fancy plots!

We'll use `corrplot` package in R which can plot a `cor` object (classical correlation matrix), or any other matrix. We will plot **MIC** matrix in this case, but any other can be used as well, for example, **MAS** or another metric that returns an squared matrix of correlations.

The two plots are based on the same data but display the correlation in different ways.

```
# library wto plot that matrix
library(corrplot)
```

```
## corrplot 0.84 loaded
```

```
# to use the color pallete brewer.pal
library(RColorBrewer)
```

```
# hack to visualize the maximum value of the
# scale excluding the diagonal (variable against itself)
diag(mine_res_hd$MIC)=0
```

```
# Correlation plot with circles.
corrplot(mine_res_hd$MIC,
         method="circle",
         col=brewer.pal(n=10, name="PuOr"),
         # only display upper diagonal
         type="lower",
         #label color, size and rotation
         tl.col="red",
         tl.cex = 0.9,
         tl.srt=90,
         # dont print diagonal (var against itself)
         diag=FALSE,
         # accept a any matrix, mic in this case
         #(not a correlation element)
         is.corr = F
```

)

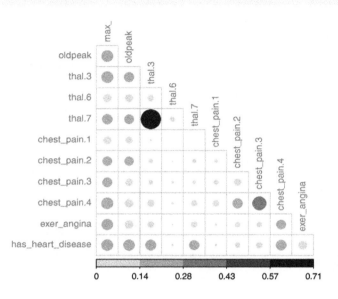

Figure 17: Correlation plot

```
# Correlation plot with color and correlation MIC
corrplot(mine_res_hd$MIC,
        method="color",
        type="lower",
        number.cex=0.7,
        # Add coefficient of correlation
        addCoef.col = "black",
        tl.col="red",
        tl.srt=90,
        tl.cex = 0.9,
        diag=FALSE,
        is.corr = F
```

)

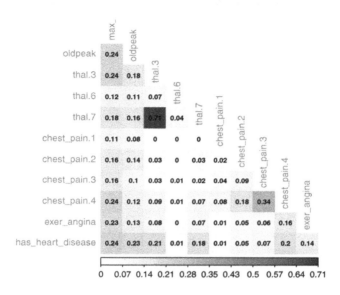

Figure 18: Correlation plot

Just change the first parameter **-mine_res_hd$MIC-** to the matrix you want and reuse with your data.

1.2.9.2 A comment about this kind of plots

They are useful only when the number of variables are not big. Or if you perform a variable selection first, keeping in mind that every variable should be numerical.

If there is some categorical variable in the selection you can convert it into numerical first and inspect the relationship between the variables, thus sneak peak how certain values in categorical variables are more related to certain outcomes, like in this case.

1.2.9.3 How about some insights from the plots?

Since the variable to predict is `has_heart_disease`, it appears something interesting, to have a heart disease is more correlated to `thal=3` than to value `thal=6`.

Same analysis for variable `chest_pain`, a value of 4 is more dangerous than a value of 1.

And we can check it with other plot:

```
cross_plot(heart_disease, input = "chest_pain",
  target = "has_heart_disease", plot_type = "percentual")
```

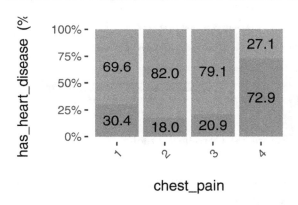

Figure 19: Visual analysis using cross-plot

The likelihood of having a heart disease is 72.9% if the patient has `chest_pain=4`. More than 2x more likely if she/(he) has `chest_pain=1` (72.9 vs 30.4%).

Some thoughts. . .

The data is the same, but the approach to browse it is different. The same goes when we are creating a predictive model, the input data in the *N-dimensional* space can be approached through different models like support vector machine, a random forest, etc.

Like a photographer shooting from different angles, or different cameras. The object is always the same, but the perspective gives different information.

Combining raw tables plus different plots gives us a more real and complementary object perspective.

1.2.10   Correlation analysis based on information theory

Based on MIC measure, mine function can receive the index of the column to predict (or to get all the correlations against only one variable).

```
# Getting the index of the variable to
# predict: has_heart_disease
target="has_heart_disease"
index_target=grep(target, colnames(heart_disease_4))


# master takes the index column number to calculate all
# the correlations
mic_predictive=mine(heart_disease_4,
                    master = index_target)$MIC


# creating the data frame containing the results,
# ordering descently by its correlation and excluding
# the correlation of target vs itself
df_predictive =
  data.frame(variable=rownames(mic_predictive),
                        mic=mic_predictive[,1],
                        stringsAsFactors = F) %>%
  arrange(-mic) %>%
```

```
filter(variable!=target)

# creating a colorful plot showing importance variable
# based on MIC measure
ggplot(df_predictive,
       aes(x=reorder(variable, mic),y=mic, fill=variable)
       ) +
  geom_bar(stat='identity') +
  coord_flip() +
  theme_bw() +
  xlab("") +
  ylab("Variable Importance (based on MIC)") +
  guides(fill=FALSE)
```

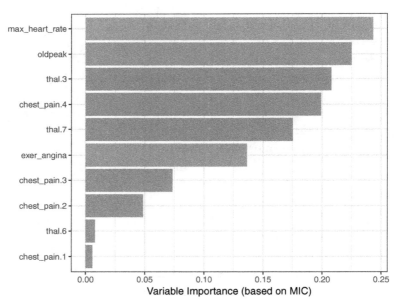

Figure 20: Correlation using information theory

Although it is recommended to run correlations among all variables in order to exclude correlated input features.

1.2.10.1   Practice advice for using `mine`

If it lasts too much time to finish, consider taking a sample. If the amount of data is too little, consider setting a higher number in `alpha` parameter, 0.6 is its default. Also, it can be run in parallel, just setting `n.cores=3` in case you have 4 cores. A general good practice when running parallel processes, the extra core will be used by the operating system.

1.2.11   But just MINE covers this?

No. We used only MINE suite, but there are other algortihms related to mutual information[23]. In R some of the packages are: entropy[24] and infotheo[25].

Package `funModeling` (from version 1.6.6) introduces the function `var_rank_info` which calculates several information theory metrics, as it was seen in section Rank best features using information theory.

In **Python** mutual information can be calculated through scikit-learn, here an example[26].

The concept transcends the tool.

1.2.11.1   Another correlation example (mutual information)

---

[23]http://www.scholarpedia.org/article/Mutual_information

[24]https://cran.r-project.org/web/packages/entropy/entropy.pdf

[25]https : / / artax . karlin . mff . cuni . cz / r - help / library / infotheo / html / mutinformation.html

[26]stackoverflow.com/questions/20491028/optimal-way-to-compute-pairwise-mutual-information-using-numpy

This time we'll use **infotheo** package, we need first to do a **data preparation** step, applying a **discretize** function (or binning) function present in the package. It converts every numerical variable into categorical based on equal frequency criteria.

Next code will create the correlation matrix as we seen before, but based on the mutual information index.

```
library(infotheo)
# discretizing every variable
heart_disease_4_disc = discretize(heart_disease_4)

# calculating 'correlation' based on mutual information
heart_info = mutinformation(heart_disease_4_disc,
  method = "emp")

# hack to visualize the maximum value of the scale
# excluding the diagonal (var against itself)
diag(heart_info) = 0

# Correlation plot with color and correlation Mutual
# Information from Infotheo package. This line only
# retrieves the plot of the right.
corrplot(heart_info, method = "color", type = "lower",
  number.cex = 0.6, addCoef.col = "black", tl.col = "red",
  tl.srt = 90, tl.cex = 0.9, diag = FALSE, is.corr = F)
```

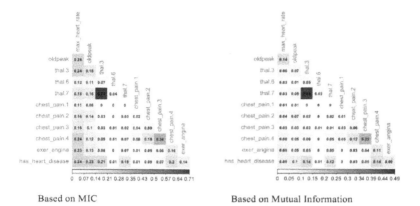

Based on MIC   Based on Mutual Information

Figure 21: Comparing variable importance

Correlation score based on mutual information ranks relationships pretty similar to MIC, doesn't it?

1.2.12   Information Measures: A general perspective

Further than correlation, MIC or other information metric measure if there is a *functional relationship*.

A high MIC value indicates that the relationship between the two variables can be explained by a function. Is our job to find that function or predictive model.

This analysis is extended to n-variables, this book introduces another algorithm in the selecting best variables chapter.

Some predictive models perform better than other, but if the relationship is absolutely noisy no matter how advance the algorithm is, it will end up in bad results.

More to come on **Information Theory**. By now you check these didactical lectures:

- 7-min introductory video https://www.youtube.com/watch?v=2s3aJfRr9gE
- http://alex.smola.org/teaching/cmu2013-10-701x/slides/R8-information_theory.pdf
- http://www.scholarpedia.org/article/Mutual_information

1.2.13 Conclusions

Anscombe's quartet taught us the good practice of getting the *raw statistic* together with a plot.

We could see how **noise** can affect the relationship between two variables, and this phenomenon always appears in data. Noise in data confuses the predictive model.

Noise is related to error, and it can be studied with measures based on information theory such as **mutual information** and **maximal information coefficient**, which go one further step than typical R squared. There is a clinical study which uses MINE as feature selector in (Caban et al. 2012).

These methods are applicable in **feature engineering** as a method which does not rely on a predictive model to rank most important variables. Also applicable to cluster time series.

Next recommended chapter: Selecting best variables

Data Science Live Book

2 Data Preparation

2.1 Handling Data Types

2.1.1 What is this about?

One of the first things to do when we start a data project is to assign the correct data type for each variable. Although this seems a straightforward task, some algorithms work with certain data types. Here, we'll try to cover these conversions while explaining with examples the implications in each case.

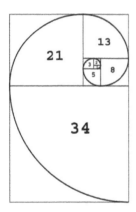

Figure 22: Fibonacci spiral

The Fibonacci series. A sequence of numbers present in nature and human bodies.

What are we going to review in this chapter?

- Detecting the correct data type
- How to convert from categorical to numerical
- How to convert from numerical to categorical (discretization methods)
- Theoretical and practical aspects (examples in R)
- How a predictive model looks at numerical variables

2.1.2   The universe of data types

There are two main data types, **numerical** and **categorical**. Other names for categorical are **string** and **nominal**.

A subset of categorical is the ordinal or, as it is named in R, an **ordered** factor. At least in R, this type is only relevant when plotting categories in a certain order. An example in R:

```
# Creating an ordinal or ordered factor
var_factor = factor(c("3_high", "2_mid", "1_low"))
var_ordered = factor(var_factor, ordered = T)
var_ordered
```

```
## [1] 3_high 2_mid  1_low
## Levels: 1_low < 2_mid < 3_high
```

Don't pay too much attention to this data type as numerical and categorical are the most needed.

2.1.2.1   Binary variable, numerical, or categorical?

This book suggests using binary variables as numeric when 0 is FALSE and 1 is TRUE. This makes it easier to profile data.

2.1.3 Data types per algorithm

Some algorithms work as follows:

- ⊞ Only with categorical data
- ✎ Only with numerical data
- ⊞ ✎ With both types

Moreover, not every predictive model can handle **missing value**.

The **Data Science Live Book** tries to cover all of these situations.

2.1.4 Converting categorical variables into numerical

Using the `caret` package in R is a straightforward task that converts every categorical variable into a **flag one**, also known as a *dummy* variable.

If the original categorical variable has thirty possible values, then it will result in 30 new columns holding the value 0 or 1, where 1 represents the presence of that category in the row.

If we use the caret package from R, then this conversion only takes two lines of code:

```
library(caret)    # contains dummyVars function
library(dplyr)    # data munging library
library(funModeling)  # df_status function

# Checking categorical variables
status = df_status(heart_disease, print_results = F)
filter(status, type %in% c("factor", "character")) %>%
  select(variable)

##            variable
## 1            gender
```

73

```
## 2              chest_pain
## 3 fasting_blood_sugar
## 4        resting_electro
## 5                   thal
## 6            exter_angina
## 7      has_heart_disease
```

```r
# It converts all categorical variables (factor and
# character) into numerical variables It skips the
# original variable, so no need to remove it after the
# conversion, the data is ready to use.
dmy = dummyVars(" ~ .", data = heart_disease)
heart_disease_2 = data.frame(predict(dmy,
  newdata = heart_disease))

# Checking the new numerical data set:
colnames(heart_disease_2)
```

```
##  [1] "age"                    "gender.female"
##  [3] "gender.male"            "chest_pain.1"
##  [5] "chest_pain.2"           "chest_pain.3"
##  [7] "chest_pain.4"           "resting_blood_pressure"
##  [9] "serum_cholestoral"      "fasting_blood_sugar.0"
## [11] "fasting_blood_sugar.1"  "resting_electro.0"
## [13] "resting_electro.1"      "resting_electro.2"
## [15] "max_heart_rate"         "exer_angina"
## [17] "oldpeak"                "slope"
## [19] "num_vessels_flour"      "thal.3"
## [21] "thal.6"                 "thal.7"
## [23] "heart_disease_severity" "exter_angina.0"
## [25] "exter_angina.1"         "has_heart_disease.no"
## [27] "has_heart_disease.yes"
```

Original data heart_disease has been converted into heart_disease_2 with no categorical variables, only numerical and dummy. Note that every new variable has a *dot* followed by the *value*.

If we check the before and after for the 7th patient (row) in variable `chest_pain` which can take the values 1, 2, 3 or 4, then

```
# before
as.numeric(heart_disease[7, "chest_pain"])
```

```
## [1] 4
```

```
# after
heart_disease_2[7, c("chest_pain.1", "chest_pain.2",
  "chest_pain.3", "chest_pain.4")]
```

```
##   chest_pain.1 chest_pain.2 chest_pain.3 chest_pain.4
## 7            0            0            0            1
```

Having kept and transformed only numeric variables while excluding the nominal ones, the data `heart_disease_2` are ready to be used.

More info about **dummyVars**: http://amunategui.github.io/dummyVar-Walkthrough/

2.1.5   Is it categorical or numerical? Think about it.

Consider the `chest_pain` variable, which can take values 1, 2, 3, or 4. Is this variable categorical or numerical?

If the values are ordered, then it can be considered as numerical as it exhibits an **order** i.e., 1 is less than 2, 2 is less than 3, and 3 is less than 4.

If we create a decision tree model, then we may find rules like: "`If chest_pain > 2.5, then...`". Does it make sense? The algorithm splits the variable by a value that is not present (`2.5`); however, the interpretation by us is "if `chest_pain` is equal or higher than 3, then...".

75

2.1.5.1 Thinking as an algorithm

Consider two numerical input variables and a target binary variable. The algorithm will *see* both input variables as dots in a rectangle, considering that there are infinite values between each number.

For example, a **Supported Vector Machine** (SVM) will create *several* vectors in order to separate the target variable class. It will **find regions** based on these vectors. How would it be possible to find these regions based on categorical variables? It isn't possible and that's why SVM only supports numerical variables as with artificial neural networks.

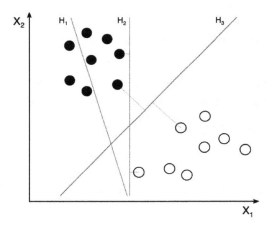

Figure 23: Support Vector Machine

Image credit: ZackWeinberg

The last image shows three lines, representing three different decision boundaries or regions.

For a quick introduction to this SVM concept, please go to this short video: SVM Demo[27].

However, if the model is tree-based, like decision trees, random forest, or gradient boosting machine, then they handle both types because their search space can be regions (same as SVM) and categories. Like the rule "`if postal_code is AX441AG and age > 55, then...`".

Going back to the heart disease example, the variable `chest_pain` exhibits order. We should take advantage of this because if we convert this to a categorical variable, then **we are losing information** and this is an important point when handling data types.

2.1.5.2   Is the solution to treat all as categorical?

No... A numerical variable carries more information than a nominal one because of its order. In categorical variables, the values cannot be compared. Let's say it's not possible to make a rule like `If postal code is higher than "AX2004-P"`.

The values of a nominal variable can be compared if we have another variable to use as a reference (usually an outcome to predict).

For example, postal code "AX2004-P" is *higher* than "MA3942-H" because there are more people interested in attending photography lessons.

In addition, **high cardinallity** is an issue in categorical variables, e.g., a `postal code` variable containing hundreds of different values. This book has addressed this in both chapters: handling high categorical variable for descriptive statistics and **when we do** predictive modelling.

Anyway, you can do the *free test* of converting all variables into categorical ones and see what happens. Compare the results with the numerical variables. Remember to use some good error measure for the test, like Kappa or ROC statistic, and to cross-validate the results.

---

[27] https://www.youtube.com/watch?v=1NxnPkZM9bc

2.1.5.3 Be aware when converting categorical into numerical variables

Imagine we have a categorical variable that we need to convert to numerical. As in the previous case, but trying a different **transformation** assign a different number to each category.

We have to be careful when doing such transformations because we are **introducing order** to the variable.

Consider the following data example having four rows. The first two variables are `visits` and `postal_code` (this works as either two input variables or `visits` as input and `postal_code` as output).

The following code will show the `visits` depending on `postal_code` transformed according to two criteria:

- `transformation_1`: Assign a sequence number based on the given order.
- `transformation_2`: Assign a number based on the number of visits.

```
# creating data -toy- sample
df_pc = data.frame(visits = c(10, 59, 27,
    33), postal_code = c("AA1", "BA5", "CG3",
    "HJ1"), transformation_1 = c(1, 2, 3,
    4), transformation_2 = c(1, 4, 2, 3))
```

```
# printing table
knitr::kable(df_pc)
```

visits	postal_code	transformation_1	transformation_2
10	AA1	1	1
59	BA5	2	4
27	CG3	3	2
33	HJ1	4	3

```r
library(gridExtra)

# transformation 1
plot_1 = ggplot(df_pc, aes(x = transformation_1,
  y = visits, label = postal_code)) +
  geom_point(aes(color = postal_code),
    size = 4) + geom_smooth(method = loess,
  group = 1, se = FALSE, color = "lightblue",
  linetype = "dashed") + theme_minimal() +
  theme(legend.position = "none") +
  geom_label(aes(fill = factor(postal_code)),
    colour = "white", fontface = "bold")


# transformation 2
plot_2 = ggplot(df_pc, aes(x = transformation_2,
  y = visits, label = postal_code)) +
  geom_point(aes(color = postal_code),
    size = 4) + geom_smooth(method = lm,
  group = 1, se = FALSE, color = "lightblue",
  linetype = "dashed") + theme_minimal() +
  theme(legend.position = "none") +
  geom_label(aes(fill = factor(postal_code)),
    colour = "white", fontface = "bold")

# arranging plots side-by-side
grid.arrange(plot_1, plot_2, ncol = 2)
```

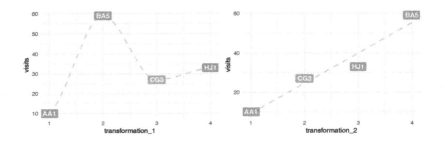

Figure 24: Data transformations comparison

To be sure, nobody builds a predictive model using only four rows; however, the intention of this example is to show how the relationship changes from non-linear (`transformation_1`) to linear (`transformation_2`). This makes things easier for the predictive model and explains the relationship.

This effect is the same when we handle millions of rows of data and the number of variables scales to hundreds. Learning from small data is a right approach in these cases.

2.1.6 Discretizing numerical variables

This process converts data into one category by splitting it into bins. For a fancy definition, we can quote *Wikipedia*: *Discretization concerns the process of transferring continuous functions, models, and equations into discrete counterparts.*

Bins are also known as buckets or segments. Let's continue with the examples.

2.1.6.1 About the data

80

The data contain information regarding the percentage of children that are stunted. The ideal value is zero.

> The indicator reflects the share of children younger than 5 years who suffer from stunting. Children with stunted growth are at greater risk for illness and death.

Data source: ourworldindata.org, hunger and undernourishment[28].

First of all, we have to do a quick **data preparation**. Each row represents a country–year pair, so we have to obtain the most recent indicator per country.

```
data_stunting=read.csv(file = "https://goo.gl/hFEUfN",
                       header = T,
                       stringsAsFactors = F)


# renaming the metric
data_stunting=
  dplyr::rename(
    data_stunting,
    share_stunted_child=
      Share.of.stunted.children.under.5
  )


# doing the grouping mentioned before
d_stunt_grp = group_by(data_stunting, Entity) %>%
  filter(Year == max(Year)) %>%
  dplyr::summarise(share_stunted_child=
                     max(share_stunted_child)
                  )
```

The most standard binning criteria are:

---

[28]https : / / ourworldindata . org / hunger - and - undernourishment / #undernourishment-of-children

- Equal range
- Equal frequency
- Custom bins

There are all explained below.

2.1.6.2 Equal range

The range is commonly found in histograms looking at distribution, but is highly susceptible to outliers. To create, for example, four bins, requires the min and max values divided by 4.

```r
# funModeling contains equal_freq (discretization)
library(funModeling)

# ggplot2 it provides 'cut_interval' function used to
# split the variables based on equal range criteria
library(ggplot2)

# Creating equal range variable, add `dig.lab=9`
# parameter to deactivate scientific notation as with
# the `cut` function.
d_stunt_grp$share_stunted_child_eq_range=
  cut_interval(d_stunt_grp$share_stunted_child, n = 4)

# The 'describe' function from Hmisc package is
# extremely useful to profile data
describe(d_stunt_grp$share_stunted_child_eq_range)

## d_stunt_grp$share_stunted_child_eq_range
##          n  missing distinct
##        154        0        4
##
## Value        [1.3,15.8] (15.8,30.3] (30.3,44.8]
```

```
## Frequency                   62              45             37
## Proportion               0.403           0.292          0.240
##
## Value          (44.8,59.3]
## Frequency               10
## Proportion            0.065
# Plotting the variable
p2=ggplot(d_stunt_grp,
          aes(share_stunted_child_eq_range)
          ) +
  geom_bar(fill="#009E73") +
  theme_bw()
p2
```

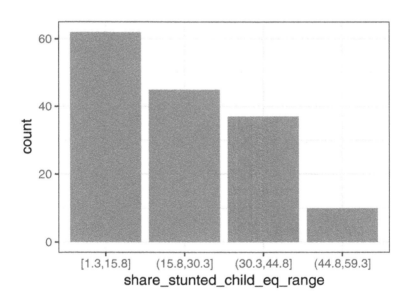

Figure 25: Equal frequency discretization

The `describe` output tells us that there are four categories in the variable and, between parenthesis/square bracket, the total number of cases per category in both absolute and relative values, respectively. For example, the category (15.8,30.3] contains all the cases that have `share_stunted_child` from 15.8 (not inclusive) to 30.3 (inclusive). It appears 45 times and represents 29% of total cases.

2.1.6.3   Equal frequency

This technique groups the same number of observations using criteria based on percentiles. More information about percentiles at Annex 1: The magic of percentiles chapter.

The `funModeling` package includes the `equal_freq` function to create bins based on these criteria:

```
d_stunt_grp$stunt_child_ef=
  equal_freq(var = d_stunt_grp$share_stunted_child,
             n_bins = 4
             )

# profiling variable
describe(d_stunt_grp$stunt_child_ef)

## d_stunt_grp$stunt_child_ef
##         n  missing distinct
##       154        0        4
##
## Value       [ 1.3, 9.5) [ 9.5,20.8) [20.8,32.9)
## Frequency            40          37          39
## Proportion        0.260       0.240       0.253
##
## Value       [32.9,59.3]
## Frequency            38
```

```
## Proportion        0.247
```

```
p3=ggplot(d_stunt_grp, aes(stunt_child_ef)) +
  geom_bar(fill="#CC79A7") + theme_bw()
p3
```

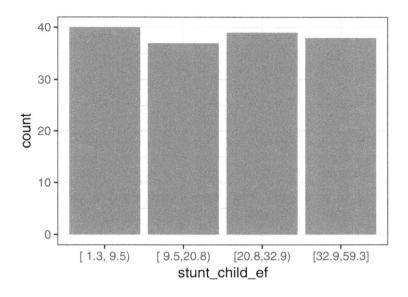

Figure 26: Equal frequency example

In this case, we select four bins so that each bin will contain an approximate 25% share.

2.1.6.4 Custom bins

If we already have the points for which we want the segments, we can use the cut function.

```
# parameter dig.lab "disable" scientific notation
d_stunt_grp$share_stunted_child_custom=
  cut(d_stunt_grp$share_stunted_child,
      breaks = c(0, 2, 9.4, 29, 100)
      )

describe(d_stunt_grp$share_stunted_child_custom)

## d_stunt_grp$share_stunted_child_custom
##         n  missing distinct
##       154        0        4
##
## Value          (0,2]   (2,9.4] (9.4,29] (29,100]
## Frequency          5        35       65       49
## Proportion     0.032     0.227    0.422    0.318
p4=ggplot(d_stunt_grp, aes(share_stunted_child_custom)) +
  geom_bar(fill="#0072B2") +
  theme_bw()
p4
```

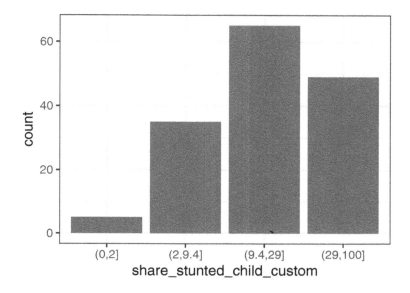

Figure 27: Manual discretization

Please note it's only needed to define the maximum value per bucket.

In general, we don't know the minimum nor maximum value. In those cases, we can use the values -Inf and Inf. Otherwise, if we define a value out of the range, cut will assign the NA value.

It's good practice to assign the minimum and maximum using a function. In this case, the variable is a percentage, so we know beforehand its scale is from 0 to 100; however, ⚠ *what would happen if we did not know the range?*

The function will return NA for those values below or above the cut points. One solution is to get variable min and max values:

```
# obtaining the min and max
min_value=min(d_stunt_grp$share_stunted_child)
max_value=max(d_stunt_grp$share_stunted_child)

# set `include.lowest=T` to include the min value,
# otherwise it will be assigned as NA.
d_stunt_grp$share_stunted_child_custom_2=
  cut(d_stunt_grp$share_stunted_child,
      breaks = c(min_value, 2, 9.4, 29, max_value),
      include.lowest = T)

describe(d_stunt_grp$share_stunted_child_custom_2)

## d_stunt_grp$share_stunted_child_custom_2
##          n  missing distinct
##        154        0        4
##
## Value       [1.3,2]   (2,9.4]  (9.4,29]  (29,59.3]
## Frequency         5        35        65         49
## Proportion    0.032     0.227     0.422      0.318
```

2.1.7   Discretization with new data

All of these transformations are made given a training dataset based
on the variables' distributions. Such is the case of equal frequency
and equal range discretization. *But what would it happen if new data
arrive?*

If a new min or max value appears, then it will affect the bin range in
the **equal range** method. If any new value arrives, then it will move
the points based on percentiles as we saw in the **equal frequency**
method.

As an example, imagine that in the proposed example we add four more cases with values 88, 2, 7 and 3:

```
# Simulating that four new values arrive
updated_data = c(d_stunt_grp$share_stunted_child, 88, 2,
  7, 3)

# discretization by equal frequency
updated_data_eq_freq = equal_freq(updated_data, 4)

# results in...
describe(updated_data_eq_freq)

## updated_data_eq_freq
##          n  missing distinct
##        158        0        4
##
## Value      [ 1.3, 9.3) [ 9.3,20.6) [20.6,32.9)
## Frequency           40          39          40
## Proportion       0.253       0.247       0.253
##
## Value      [32.9,88.0]
## Frequency           39
## Proportion       0.247
```

Now we compare with the bins we created before:

```
describe(d_stunt_grp$stunt_child_ef)

## d_stunt_grp$stunt_child_ef
##          n  missing distinct
##        154        0        4
##
## Value      [ 1.3, 9.5) [ 9.5,20.8) [20.8,32.9)
## Frequency           40          37          39
```

```
## Proportion         0.260        0.240        0.253
##
## Value        [32.9,59.3]
## Frequency              38
## Proportion        0.247
```

All the bins changed! 😱Because these are new categories, the predictive model will fail to handle them because they are all new values.

The solution is to save the cut points when we do data preparation. Then, when we run the model on production, we use the custom bin discretization and, thereby, force every new case in the proper category. This way, the predictive model will always *sees* the same.

The solution in next section.

2.1.8   Automatic data frame discretization

The package `funModeling` (from version > 1.6.6) introduces two functions— `discretize_get_bins` & `discretize_df` —that work together in order to help us in the discretization task.

```
# First we load the libraries
# install.packages('funModeling')
library(funModeling)
library(dplyr)
```

Let's see an example. First, we check current data types:

```
df_status(heart_disease, print_results = F) %>%
   select(variable, type, unique, q_na) %>% arrange(type)
```

```
##                   variable    type unique q_na
## 1                   gender  factor      2    0
## 2               chest_pain  factor      4    0
```

90

```
## 3        fasting_blood_sugar  factor      2    0
## 4         resting_electro     factor      3    0
## 5                    thal     factor      3    2
## 6            exter_angina     factor      2    0
## 7       has_heart_disease     factor      2    0
## 8                     age   integer     41    0
## 9   resting_blood_pressure  integer     50    0
## 10        serum_cholestoral integer    152    0
## 11          max_heart_rate  integer     91    0
## 12             exer_angina  integer      2    0
## 13                   slope  integer      3    0
## 14        num_vessels_flour integer      4    4
## 15 heart_disease_severity   integer      5    0
## 16                 oldpeak  numeric     40    0
```

We've got factor, integer, and numeric variables: a good mix! The transformation has two steps. First, it gets the cuts or threshold values from which each segment begins. The second step is using the threshold to obtain the variables as categoricals.

Two variables will be discretized in the following example: `max_heart_rate` and `oldpeak`. Also, we'll introduce some `NA` values into `oldpeak` to test how the function works with missing data.

```
# creating a copy to keep original data clean
heart_disease_2 = heart_disease
```

```
# Introducing some missing values in the first 30 rows of
# the oldpeak variable
heart_disease_2$oldpeak[1:30] = NA
```

Step 1) Getting the bin thresholds for each input variable:

`discretize_get_bins` returns a data frame that needs to be used in the `discretize_df` function, which returns the final processed data frame.

```
d_bins = discretize_get_bins(data = heart_disease_2,
  input = c("max_heart_rate", "oldpeak"), n_bins = 5)
```

```
## [1] "Variables processed: max_heart_rate, oldpeak"
# Checking `d_bins` object:
d_bins
```

```
##            variable               cuts
## 1 max_heart_rate 131|147|160|171|Inf
## 2        oldpeak   0.1|0.3|1.1|2|Inf
```

Parameters:

- **data**: the data frame containing the variables to be processed.
- **input**: vector of strings containing the variable names.
- **n_bins**: the number of bins/segments to have in the discretized data.

We can see each threshold point (or upper boundary) for each variable.

Note: Changes from version 1.6.6 to 1.6.7:

- **discretize_get_bins** doesn't create the -Inf threshold since that value was always considered to be the minimum.
- The one value category now it is represented as a range, for example, what it was "5", now it is "[5, 6)".
- Buckets formatting may have changed, if you were using this function in production, you would need to check the new values.

Time to continue with next step!

Step 2) Applying the thresholds for each variable:

```
# Now it can be applied on the same data frame or in
# a new one (for example, in a predictive model that
# changes data over time)
```

```
heart_disease_discretized =
  discretize_df(data=heart_disease_2,
                data_bins=d_bins,
                stringsAsFactors=T)
```

[1] "Variables processed: max_heart_rate, oldpeak"

Parameters:

- `data`: data frame containing the numerical variables to be discretized.
- `data_bins`: data frame returned by `discretize_get_bins`. If it is changed by the user, then each upper boundary must be separated by a pipe character (|) as shown in the example.
- `stringsAsFactors`: TRUE by default, final variables will be factor (instead of a character) and useful when plotting.

2.1.8.1 Final results and their plots

Before and after:

```
##    max_heart_rate_before max_heart_rate_after
## 1                    171          [ 171, Inf]
## 2                    114          [-Inf, 131)
## 3                    151          [ 147, 160)
## 4                    160          [ 160, 171)
## 5                    158          [ 147, 160)
## 6                    161          [ 160, 171)
##    oldpeak_before oldpeak_after
## 1             NA            NA.
## 2             NA            NA.
## 3            1.8   [ 1.1, 2.0)
## 4            1.4   [ 1.1, 2.0)
## 5            0.0   [-Inf, 0.1)
```

93

```
## 6                 0.5    [ 0.3, 1.1)
```

Final distribution:

```
freq(heart_disease_discretized %>%
         select(max_heart_rate,oldpeak),
      plot = F)
```

```
##    max_heart_rate frequency percentage cumulative_perc
## 1     [-Inf, 131)        63      20.79           20.79
## 2     [ 147, 160)        62      20.46           41.25
## 3     [ 160, 171)        62      20.46           61.71
## 4     [ 131, 147)        59      19.47           81.18
## 5     [ 171, Inf]        57      18.81          100.00
##
##          oldpeak frequency percentage cumulative_perc
## 1 [-Inf, 0.1)           97      32.01           32.01
## 2 [ 0.3, 1.1)           54      17.82           49.83
## 3 [ 1.1, 2.0)           54      17.82           67.65
## 4 [ 2.0, Inf]           50      16.50           84.15
## 5         NA.           30       9.90           94.05
## 6 [ 0.1, 0.3)           18       5.94          100.00
```

```
## [1] "Variables processed: max_heart_rate, oldpeak"
```

```
p5=ggplot(heart_disease_discretized,
          aes(max_heart_rate)) +
  geom_bar(fill="#0072B2") +
  theme_bw() +
  theme(axis.text.x =
          element_text(angle = 45, vjust = 1, hjust=1)
        )

p6=ggplot(heart_disease_discretized,
          aes(oldpeak)) +
```

```
geom_bar(fill="#CC79A7") +
theme_bw() +
theme(axis.text.x =
        element_text(angle = 45, vjust = 1, hjust=1)
    )
```

```
gridExtra::grid.arrange(p5, p6, ncol=2)
```

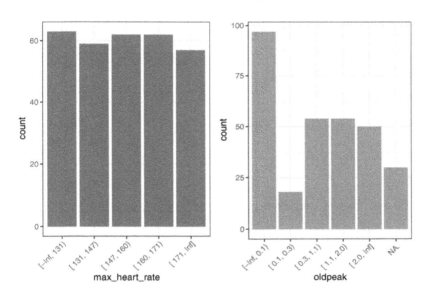

Figure 28: Automatic discretization results

Sometimes, it is not possible to get the same number of cases per bucket when computing **equal frequency** as is shown in the `oldpeak` variable.

2.1.8.2   NA handling

Regarding the NA values, the new `oldpeak` variable has six categories: five categories defined in `n_bins=5` plus the `NA.` value. Note the point at the end indicating the presence of missing values.

2.1.8.3 More info

- `discretize_df` will never return an NA value without transforming it to the string `NA.`.
- `n_bins` sets the number of bins for all the variables.
- If `input` is missing, then it will run for all numeric/integer variables whose number of unique values is greater than the number of bins (`n_bins`).
- Only the variables defined in `input` will be processed while remaining variables will **not be modified at all**.
- `discretize_get_bins` returns just a data frame that can be changed by hand as needed, either in a text file or in the R session.

2.1.8.4 Discretization with new data

In our data, the minimum value for `max_heart_rate` is 71. The data preparation must be robust with new data; e.g., if a new patient arrives whose `max_heart_rate` is 68, then the current process will assign her/him to the lowest category.

In other functions from other packages, this preparation may return an NA because it is out of the segment.

As we pointed out before, if new data comes over time, it's likely to get new min/max value/s. This can break our process. To solve this, `discretize_df` will always have as min/max the values `-Inf`/`Inf`; thus, any new value falling below/above the minimum/maximum will be added to the lowest or highest segment as applicable.

The data frame returned by `discretize_get_bins` must be saved in order to apply it to new data. If the discretization is not intended to run with new data, then there is no sense in having two functions: it can be only one. In addition, there would be no need to save the results of `discretize_get_bins`.

Having this two-step approach, we can handle both cases.

2.1.8.5 Conclusions about two-step discretization

The usage of `discretize_get_bins` + `discretize_df` provides quick data preparation, with a clean data frame that is ready to use. Clearly showing where each segment begin and end, indispensable when making statistical reports.

The decision of *not fail* when dealing with a new min/max in new data is **just a decision**. In some contexts, failure would be the desired behavior.

The human intervention: The easiest way to discretize a data frame is to select the same number of bins to apply to every variable—just like the example we saw—however, if tuning is needed, then some variables may need a **different number of bins**. For example, a variable with less dispersion can work well with a low number of bins.

Common values for the number of segments could be 3, 5, 10, or 20 (but no more). It is up to the data scientist to make this decision.

2.1.8.6 Bonus track: The trade-off art ⚖️

- A high number of bins => More noise captured.
- A low number of bins => Oversimplification, less variance.

Do these terms sound similar to any other ones in machine learning?

The answer: **Yes!**. Just to mention one example: the trade-off between adding or subtracting variables from a predictive model.

- More variables: Overfitting alert (too detailed predictive model).
- Fewer variables: Underfitting danger (not enough information to capture general patterns).

Just like oriental philosophy has pointed out for thousands of years, there is an art in finding the right balance between one value and its opposite.

2.1.9   Final thoughts

As we can see, **there is no free lunch** in discretization or data preparation. How do you think that an *automatic or intelligent system* will handle all of these situations without human intervention or analysis?

To be sure, we can delegate some tasks to automatic processes; however, **humans are indispensable in data preparation stage**, giving the correct input data to process.

The assignment of variables as categorical or numerical, the two most used data types varies according to the nature of the data and the selected algorithms as some only support one data type.

The conversion **introduces some bias** to the analysis. A similar case exists when we deal with missing values: Handling and Imputation of Missing Data.

When we work with categorical variables, we can change their distribution by re-arranging the categories according to a target variable in order to **better expose their relationship**. Converting a non-linear variable relationship, into one linear.

2.1.10 Bonus track ✳

Let's go back to the discretization variable section and plot all the transformations we've seen so far:

```
grid.arrange(p2, p3, p4, ncol = 3)
```

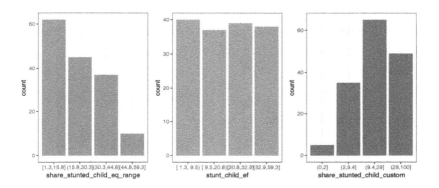

Figure 29: Same data, different visualizations

The input data is always the same. However, all of these methods **exhibit different perspectives of the same *thing*.**

Some perspectives are more suitable than others for certain situations, such as the use of **equal frequency** for **predictive modeling**.

Although this case is only considering one variable, the reasoning is the same if we have several variables at once, i.e., an `N-dimensional` space.

When we build predictive models, we describe the same bunch of points in different ways as when people give an opinion regarding some object.

2.2 High Cardinality Variable in Descriptive Stats

2.2.1 What is this about?

A **high cardinality** variable is one in which it can take *many* different values. For example country.

This chapter will cover cardinality reduction based on Pareto rule, using the `freq` function which gives a quick view about where the most of values are concentrated and variable distribution.

2.2.2 High Cardinality in Descriptive Statistics

The following example contains a survey of 910 cases, with 3 columns: `person`, `country` and `has_flu`, which indicates having such illness in the last month.

```
library(funModeling)
```

`data_country` data comes inside **funModeling** package (please update to release 1.6).

Quick `data_country` profiling (first 10 rows)

```
# plotting first 10 rows
head(data_country, 10)
```

```
##      person      country has_flu
```

100

```
## 478   478      France    no
## 990   990      Brazil    no
## 606   606      France    no
## 575   575 Philippines    no
## 806   806      France    no
## 232   232      France    no
## 422   422      Poland    no
## 347   347     Romania    no
## 858   858     Finland    no
## 704   704      France    no
```

```
# exploring data, displaying only first 10 rows
head(freq(data_country, "country"), 10)
```

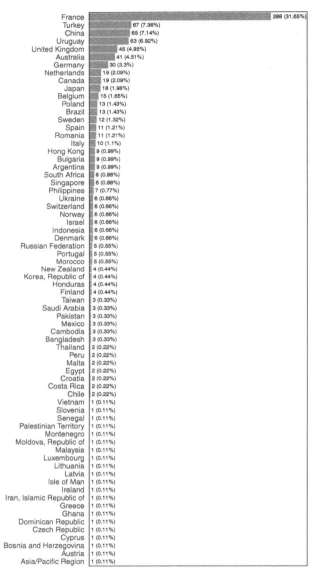

Figure 30: Country frequency analysis

```
##            country frequency percentage cumulative_perc
## 1          France       288      31.65           31.65
## 2          Turkey        67       7.36           39.01
## 3           China        65       7.14           46.15
## 4         Uruguay        63       6.92           53.07
## 5  United Kingdom        45       4.95           58.02
## 6       Australia        41       4.51           62.53
## 7         Germany        30       3.30           65.83
## 8          Canada        19       2.09           67.92
## 9     Netherlands        19       2.09           70.01
## 10          Japan        18       1.98           71.99
```
 # exploring data
freq(data_country, "has_flu")

Figure 31: Has flue frequency analysis

```
##    has_flu frequency percentage cumulative_perc
## 1       no       827      90.88           90.88
## 2      yes        83       9.12          100.00
```

The last table shows there are only 83 rows where has_flu="yes", representing around a 9% of total people.

But many of them have almost no participation in the data. This is the *long tail*, so one technique to reduce cardinality is to keep those categories that are present in a high percentage of data share, for example 70, 80 or 90%, the Pareto principle.

```
# 'freq' function, from 'funModeling' package, retrieves
# the cumulative_percentage that will help to do the cut.
country_freq = freq(data_country, "country", plot = F)

# Since 'country_freq' is an ordered table by frequency,
# let's inspect the first 10 rows with the most share.
country_freq[1:10, ]
```

```
##              country frequency percentage cumulative_perc
## 1            France       288      31.65           31.65
## 2            Turkey        67       7.36           39.01
## 3             China        65       7.14           46.15
## 4           Uruguay        63       6.92           53.07
## 5    United Kingdom        45       4.95           58.02
## 6         Australia        41       4.51           62.53
## 7           Germany        30       3.30           65.83
## 8            Canada        19       2.09           67.92
## 9       Netherlands        19       2.09           70.01
## 10            Japan        18       1.98           71.99
```

So 10 countries represent more the 70% of cases. We can assign the
category other to the remaining cases and plot:

```
data_country$country_2 = ifelse(data_country$country %in%
  country_freq[1:10, "country"], data_country$country,
  "other")
freq(data_country, "country_2")
```

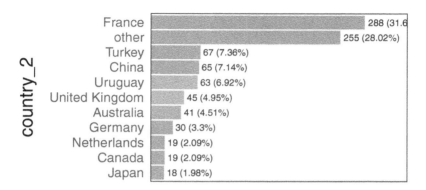

Figure 32: Modified country variable - frequency analysis

##		country_2	frequency	percentage	cumulative_perc
##	1	France	288	31.65	31.65
##	2	other	255	28.02	59.67
##	3	Turkey	67	7.36	67.03
##	4	China	65	7.14	74.17
##	5	Uruguay	63	6.92	81.09
##	6	United Kingdom	45	4.95	86.04
##	7	Australia	41	4.51	90.55
##	8	Germany	30	3.30	93.85
##	9	Canada	19	2.09	95.94
##	10	Netherlands	19	2.09	98.03
##	11	Japan	18	1.98	100.00

2.2.3 Final comments

Low representative categories are sometimes errors in data, such as
having: **Egypt**, **Eggypt.**, and may give some evidence in bad habbits

collecting data and/or possible errors when collecting from the source.

There is no general rule to shrink data, it depends on each case.

Next recommended chapter: High Cardinality Variable in Predictive Modeling.

Data Science Live Book

2.3 High Cardinality Variable in Predictive Modeling

2.3.1 What is this about?

As we've seen in the last chapter, *High Cardinality in Descriptive Statistics*, we keep the categories with the major representativeness, but how about having another variable to predict with it? That is, to predict `has_flu` based on `country`.

Using the last method may destroy the information of the variable, thus it **loses predictive power**. In this chapter we'll go further in the method described above, using an automatic grouping function -`auto_grouping`- surfing through the variable's structure, giving some ideas about how to optimize a categorical variable, but more importantly: encouraging the reader to perform her-his own optimizations.

Other literature named this re-grouping as cardinality reduction or **encoding**.

What are we going to review in this chapter?

- Concept of representativeness of data (sample size).
- Sample size having a target or outcome variable.
- From R: Present a method to help reduce cardinality and profiling categoric variable.
- A practical before-and-after example reducing cardinality and insights extraction.
- How different models such as random forest or a gradient boosting machine deals with categorical variables.

2.3.2 But is it necessary to re-group the variable?

It depends on the case, but the quickest answer is yes. In this chapter we will see one case in which this data preparation increases overall accuracy (measuring by the Area Under Roc Curve).

There is a tradeoff between the **representation of the data** (how many rows each category has), and how is each category related to the outcome variable. E.g.: some countries are more prone to cases of flu than others

```
# Loading funModeling >=1.6 which contains functions to
# deal with this.
library(funModeling)
library(dplyr)
```

Profiling **data_country**, which comes inside **funModeling** package (please update to release > 1.6.5).

Quick **data_country** profiling (first 10 rows)

```
# plotting first 10 rows
head(data_country, 10)
```

```
##      person    country has_flu country_2
```

107

```
## 478   478      France    no   France
## 990   990      Brazil    no   other
## 606   606      France    no   France
## 575   575 Philippines    no   other
## 806   806      France    no   France
## 232   232      France    no   France
## 422   422      Poland    no   other
## 347   347     Romania    no   other
## 858   858     Finland    no   other
## 704   704      France    no   France
```

```
# exploring data, displaying only first 10 rows
head(freq(data_country, "country"), 10)
```

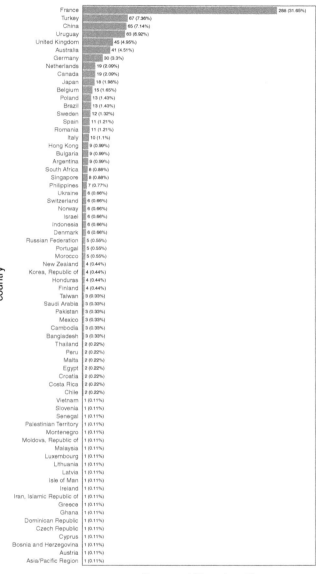

France	288 (31.65%)
Turkey	67 (7.36%)
China	65 (7.14%)
Uruguay	63 (6.92%)
United Kingdom	45 (4.95%)
Australia	41 (4.51%)
Germany	30 (3.3%)
Netherlands	19 (2.09%)
Canada	19 (2.09%)
Japan	18 (1.98%)
Belgium	15 (1.65%)
Poland	13 (1.43%)
Brazil	13 (1.43%)
Sweden	12 (1.32%)
Spain	11 (1.21%)
Romania	11 (1.21%)
Italy	10 (1.1%)
Hong Kong	9 (0.99%)
Bulgaria	9 (0.99%)
Argentina	9 (0.99%)
South Africa	8 (0.88%)
Singapore	8 (0.88%)
Philippines	7 (0.77%)
Ukraine	6 (0.66%)
Switzerland	6 (0.66%)
Norway	6 (0.66%)
Israel	6 (0.66%)
Indonesia	6 (0.66%)
Denmark	6 (0.66%)
Russian Federation	5 (0.55%)
Portugal	5 (0.55%)
Morocco	5 (0.55%)
New Zealand	4 (0.44%)
Korea, Republic of	4 (0.44%)
Honduras	4 (0.44%)
Finland	4 (0.44%)
Taiwan	3 (0.33%)
Saudi Arabia	3 (0.33%)
Pakistan	3 (0.33%)
Mexico	3 (0.33%)
Cambodia	3 (0.33%)
Bangladesh	3 (0.33%)
Thailand	2 (0.22%)
Peru	2 (0.22%)
Malta	2 (0.22%)
Egypt	2 (0.22%)
Croatia	2 (0.22%)
Costa Rica	2 (0.22%)
Chile	2 (0.22%)
Vietnam	1 (0.11%)
Slovenia	1 (0.11%)
Senegal	1 (0.11%)
Palestinian Territory	1 (0.11%)
Montenegro	1 (0.11%)
Moldova, Republic of	1 (0.11%)
Malaysia	1 (0.11%)
Luxembourg	1 (0.11%)
Lithuania	1 (0.11%)
Latvia	1 (0.11%)
Isle of Man	1 (0.11%)
Ireland	1 (0.11%)
Iran, Islamic Republic of	1 (0.11%)
Greece	1 (0.11%)
Ghana	1 (0.11%)
Dominican Republic	1 (0.11%)
Czech Republic	1 (0.11%)
Cyprus	1 (0.11%)
Bosnia and Herzegovina	1 (0.11%)
Austria	1 (0.11%)
Asia/Pacific Region	1 (0.11%)

country

Frequency / (Percentage %)

Figure 33: First 10 countries

```
##          country frequency percentage cumulative_perc
## 1          France       288      31.65           31.65
## 2          Turkey        67       7.36           39.01
## 3           China        65       7.14           46.15
## 4         Uruguay        63       6.92           53.07
## 5  United Kingdom        45       4.95           58.02
## 6       Australia        41       4.51           62.53
## 7         Germany        30       3.30           65.83
## 8          Canada        19       2.09           67.92
## 9     Netherlands        19       2.09           70.01
## 10          Japan        18       1.98           71.99
# exploring data
freq(data_country, "has_flu")
```

Figure 34: Has flu distribution

```
##   has_flu frequency percentage cumulative_perc
## 1      no       827      90.88           90.88
## 2     yes        83       9.12          100.00
```

110

2.3.3   The case 🔍

The predictive model will try to map certain values with certain outcomes, in our case the target variable is binary.

We'll computed a complete profiling of `country` regarding the target variable `has_flu` based on `categ_analysis`.

Each row represent an unique category of `input` variables. Withing each row you can find attributes that define each category in terms of representativeness and likelihood.

```
# `categ_analysis` is available in 'funModeling' >= v1.6,
# please install it before using it.
country_profiling = categ_analysis(data = data_country,
  input = "country", target = "has_flu")

# Printing first 15 rows (countries) out of 70.
head(country_profiling, 15)
```

	country	mean_target	sum_target	perc_target	q_rows	perc_rows
1	Malaysia	1.000	1	0.012	1	0.001
2	Mexico	0.667	2	0.024	3	0.003
3	Portugal	0.200	1	0.012	5	0.005
4	United Kingdom	0.178	8	0.096	45	0.049
5	Uruguay	0.175	11	0.133	63	0.069
6	Israel	0.167	1	0.012	6	0.007
7	Switzerland	0.167	1	0.012	6	0.007
8	Canada	0.158	3	0.036	19	0.021
9	France	0.142	41	0.494	288	0.316
10	Argentina	0.111	1	0.012	9	0.010
11	Germany	0.100	3	0.036	30	0.033
12	Australia	0.098	4	0.048	41	0.045
13	Romania	0.091	1	0.012	11	0.012
14	Spain	0.091	1	0.012	11	0.012
15	Sweden	0.083	1	0.012	12	0.013

Figure 35: Analyzing target vs. input

- Note 1: *The first column automatically adjusts its name based on **input** variable*
- Note 2: ***has_flu** variable has values **yes** and **no**, **categ_analysis** assigns internally the number **1** to the less representative class,*

111

yes in this case, in order to calculate the mean, sum and percentage.

These are the metrics returned by `categ_analysis`:

- `country`: name of each category in `input` variable.
- `mean_target`: `sum_target/q_rows`, average number of `has_flu="yes"` for that category. This is the likelihood.
- `sum_target`: quantity of `has_flu="yes"` values are in each category.
- `perc_target`: the same as `sum_target` but in percentage, `sum_target of each category / total sum_target`. This column sums `1.00`.
- `q_rows`: quantity of rows that, regardless of the `has_flu` variable, fell in that category. It's the distribution of `input`. This column sums the total rows analyzed.
- `perc_rows`: related to `q_rows` it represents the share or percentage of each category. This column sums `1.00`

2.3.3.1   What conclusions can we draw from this?

Reading example based on 1st `France` row:

- 41 people have flu (`sum_target=41`). These 41 people represent almost 50% of the total people having flu (`perc_target=0.494`).
- Likelihood of having flu in France is 14.2% (`mean_target=0.142`)
- Total rows from France=288 -out of 910-. This is the `q_rows` variable; `perc_rows` is the same number but in percentage.

Without considering the filter by country, we've got:

- Column `sum_target` sums the total people with flu present in data.
- Column `perc_target` sums `1.00` -or 100%

- Column `q_rows` sums total rows present in `data_country` data frame.
- Column `perc_rows` sums `1.00` -or 100%.

2.3.4 Analysis for Predictive Modeling 🌐

When developing predictive models, we may be interested in those values which increases the likelihood of a certain event. In our case:

What are the countries that maximize the likelihood of finding people with flu?

Easy, take `country_profiling` in a descending order by `mean_target`:

```
# Ordering country_profiling by mean_target and then take
# the first 6 countries
arrange(country_profiling, -mean_target) %>% head(.)
```

```
##                country mean_target sum_target perc_target
## 1             Malaysia       1.000          1       0.012
## 2               Mexico       0.667          2       0.024
## 3             Portugal       0.200          1       0.012
## 4       United Kingdom       0.178          8       0.096
## 5              Uruguay       0.175         11       0.133
## 6               Israel       0.167          1       0.012
##    q_rows perc_rows
## 1       1     0.001
## 2       3     0.003
## 3       5     0.005
## 4      45     0.049
## 5      63     0.069
## 6       6     0.007
```

113

Great! We've got `Malasyia` as the country with the highest likelihood to have flu! 100% of people there have flu (`mean_has_flu=1.000`).

But our common sense advises us that *perhaps* something is wrong...

How many rows does Malasya have? Answer: 1. -column: `q_rows=1`
How many positive cases does Malasya have? Answer: 1 -column: `sum_target=1`

Since the sample cannot be increased see if this proportion stays high, it will contribute to **overfit** and create a bias on the predictive model.

How about `Mexico`? 2 out of 3 have flu... it still seems low. However `Uruguay` has 17.3% likelihood -11 out of 63 cases- and these 63 cases represents almost 7% of total population (`perc_row=0.069`), this ratio seems more credible.

Next there are some ideas to treat this:

2.3.4.1 Case 1: Reducing by re-categorizing less representative values

Keep all cases with at least certain percentage of representation in data. Let's say to rename the countries that have less than 1% of presence in data to `others`.

```
country_profiling = categ_analysis(data = data_country,
  input = "country", target = "has_flu")

countries_high_rep = filter(country_profiling,
  perc_rows > 0.01) %>% .$country

# If not in countries_high_rep then assign `other`
# category
```

```
data_country$country_new = ifelse(data_country$country %in%
    countries_high_rep, data_country$country, "other")
```

Checking again the likelihood:

```
country_profiling_new = categ_analysis(data = data_country,
    input = "country_new", target = "has_flu")
country_profiling_new
```

```
##          country_new mean_target sum_target perc_target
## 1    United Kingdom       0.178          8       0.096
## 2           Uruguay       0.175         11       0.133
## 3            Canada       0.158          3       0.036
## 4            France       0.142         41       0.494
## 5           Germany       0.100          3       0.036
## 6         Australia       0.098          4       0.048
## 7           Romania       0.091          1       0.012
## 8             Spain       0.091          1       0.012
## 9            Sweden       0.083          1       0.012
## 10      Netherlands       0.053          1       0.012
## 11            other       0.041          7       0.084
## 12           Turkey       0.030          2       0.024
## 13          Belgium       0.000          0       0.000
## 14           Brazil       0.000          0       0.000
## 15            China       0.000          0       0.000
## 16            Italy       0.000          0       0.000
## 17            Japan       0.000          0       0.000
## 18           Poland       0.000          0       0.000
##     q_rows perc_rows
## 1       45     0.049
## 2       63     0.069
## 3       19     0.021
## 4      288     0.316
```

115

```
## 5      30     0.033
## 6      41     0.045
## 7      11     0.012
## 8      11     0.012
## 9      12     0.013
## 10     19     0.021
## 11    170     0.187
## 12     67     0.074
## 13     15     0.016
## 14     13     0.014
## 15     65     0.071
## 16     10     0.011
## 17     18     0.020
## 18     13     0.014
```

We've reduced the quantity of countries drastically -**74% less**- only by shrinking the less representative at 1%. Obtaining 18 out of 70 countries.

Likelihood of target variable has been stabilised a little more in **other** category. Now when the predictive model *sees* `Malasya` it will **not assign 100% of likelihood, but 4.1%** (`mean_has_flu=0.041`).

Advice about this last method:

Watch out about applying this technique blindly. Sometimes in a **highly unbalanced** target prediction -e.g. **anomaly detection**- the abnormal behavior is present in less than 1% of cases.

```
# replicating the data
d_abnormal = data_country

# simulating abnormal behavior with some countries
d_abnormal$abnormal = ifelse(d_abnormal$country %in%
  c("Brazil", "Chile"), "yes", "no")
```

```
# categorical analysis
ab_analysis = categ_analysis(d_abnormal,
  input = "country", target = "abnormal")

# displaying only first 6 elements
head(ab_analysis)
```

```
##                      country mean_target sum_target
## 1                     Brazil           1         13
## 2                      Chile           1          2
## 3                  Argentina           0          0
## 4 Asia/Pacific Region                   0          0
## 5                  Australia           0          0
## 6                    Austria           0          0
##   perc_target q_rows perc_rows
## 1       0.867     13     0.014
## 2       0.133      2     0.002
## 3       0.000      9     0.010
## 4       0.000      1     0.001
## 5       0.000     41     0.045
## 6       0.000      1     0.001
```

```
# inspecting distribution, just a few belongs to 'no'
# category
freq(d_abnormal, "abnormal", plot = F)
```

```
##   abnormal frequency percentage cumulative_perc
## 1       no       895      98.35           98.35
## 2      yes        15       1.65          100.00
```

How many abnormal values are there?

Only 15, and they represent 1.65% of total values.

Checking the table returned by `categ_analysis`, we can see that this *abnormal behavior* occurs **only** in categories with a really low participation: `Brazil` which is present in only 1.4% of cases, and `Chile` with 0.2%.

Creating a category `other` based on the distribution is not a good idea here.

Conclusion:

Despite the fact this is a prepared example, there are some data preparations techniques that can be really useful in terms of accuracy, but they need some supervision. This supervision can be helped by algorithms.

2.3.4.2   Case 2: Reducing by automatic grouping

This procedure uses the `kmeans` clustering technique and the table returned by `categ_analysis` in order to create groups -clusters- which contain categories which exhibit similar behavior in terms of:

- `perc_rows`
- `perc_target`

The combination of both will lead to find groups considering likelihood and representativeness.

Hands on R:

We define the `n_groups` parameter, it's the number of desired groups. The number is relative to the data and the number of total categories. But a general number would be between 3 and 10.

Function `auto_grouping` comes in `funModeling` >=1.6. Please note that the `target` parameter only supports for non binary variables.

*Note: the **seed** parameter is optional, but assigning a number will retrieve always the same results.*

```
# Reducing the cardinality
country_groups = auto_grouping(data = data_country,
  input = "country", target = "has_flu", n_groups = 9,
  seed = 999)
country_groups$df_equivalence
```

```
##                           country country_rec
## 1                       Australia     group_1
## 2                          Canada     group_1
## 3                         Germany     group_1
## 4                          France     group_2
## 5                           China     group_3
## 6                          Turkey     group_3
## 7            Asia/Pacific Region     group_4
## 8                         Austria     group_4
## 9                      Bangladesh     group_4
## 10      Bosnia and Herzegovina     group_4
## 11                       Cambodia     group_4
## 12                          Chile     group_4
## 13                     Costa Rica     group_4
## 14                        Croatia     group_4
## 15                         Cyprus     group_4
## 16                 Czech Republic     group_4
## 17             Dominican Republic     group_4
## 18                          Egypt     group_4
## 19                          Ghana     group_4
## 20                         Greece     group_4
## 21    Iran, Islamic Republic of     group_4
## 22                        Ireland     group_4
## 23                    Isle of Man     group_4
## 24                         Latvia     group_4
```

```
## 25                   Lithuania    group_4
## 26                  Luxembourg    group_4
## 27                       Malta    group_4
## 28        Moldova, Republic of    group_4
## 29                  Montenegro    group_4
## 30                    Pakistan    group_4
## 31       Palestinian Territory    group_4
## 32                        Peru    group_4
## 33                Saudi Arabia    group_4
## 34                     Senegal    group_4
## 35                    Slovenia    group_4
## 36                      Taiwan    group_4
## 37                    Thailand    group_4
## 38                     Vietnam    group_4
## 39                     Belgium    group_5
## 40                      Brazil    group_5
## 41                    Bulgaria    group_5
## 42                   Hong Kong    group_5
## 43                       Italy    group_5
## 44                      Poland    group_5
## 45                   Singapore    group_5
## 46                South Africa    group_5
## 47                   Argentina    group_6
## 48                      Israel    group_6
## 49                    Malaysia    group_6
## 50                      Mexico    group_6
## 51                    Portugal    group_6
## 52                     Romania    group_6
## 53                       Spain    group_6
## 54                      Sweden    group_6
## 55                 Switzerland    group_6
## 56                       Japan    group_7
## 57                 Netherlands    group_7
```

```
## 58           United Kingdom      group_8
## 59                  Uruguay      group_8
## 60                  Denmark      group_9
## 61                  Finland      group_9
## 62                 Honduras      group_9
## 63                Indonesia      group_9
## 64       Korea, Republic of      group_9
## 65                  Morocco      group_9
## 66              New Zealand      group_9
## 67                   Norway      group_9
## 68              Philippines      group_9
## 69       Russian Federation      group_9
## 70                  Ukraine      group_9
```

auto_grouping returns a list containing 3 objects:

- df_equivalence: data frame which contains a table to map old to new values.
- fit_cluster: k-means model used to reduce the cardinality (values are scaled).
- recateg_results: data frame containing the profiling of each group regarding target variable, first column adjusts its name to the input variable in this case we've got: country_rec. Each group correspond to one or many categories of the input variable (as seen in df_equivalence).

Let's explore how the new groups behave, this is what the predictive model will *see*:

country_groups$recateg_results

```
##    country_rec mean_target sum_target perc_target q_rows
## 1      group_8       0.176         19       0.229    108
## 2      group_6       0.156         10       0.120     64
## 3      group_2       0.142         41       0.494    288
```

```
## 4      group_1      0.111      10      0.120      90
## 5      group_7      0.027       1      0.012      37
## 6      group_3      0.015       2      0.024     132
## 7      group_4      0.000       0      0.000      49
## 8      group_5      0.000       0      0.000      85
## 9      group_9      0.000       0      0.000      57
##    perc_rows
## 1      0.119
## 2      0.070
## 3      0.316
## 4      0.099
## 5      0.041
## 6      0.145
## 7      0.054
## 8      0.093
## 9      0.063
```

Last table is ordered by `mean_target`, so we can quickly see groups maximizing and minimizing the likelihood.

- `group_2` is the most common, it is present in 31.6% of cases and `mean_target` (likelihood) is 14.2%.
- `group_8` has the highest likelihood (17.6%). Followed by `group_6` with chance of 15.6% of having a positive case (`has_flu="yes"`).
- `group_4`, `group_5` and `group_9` looks the same. They can be one group since likelihood is 0 in all the cases.
- `group_7` and `group_3` have 1 and 2 countries with positive cases. We could consider these numbers as the same, grouping them into one group, which in the end will represent the countries with the lowest likelihood.

First we need to add the new category column to the original dataset.

```
data_country_2 = data_country %>%
  inner_join(country_groups$df_equivalence,
```

```
  by = "country")
```

Now we do the additional transformations replacing:

- group_4, group_5 and group_9 will be low_likelihood, (countries with no positive cases or low target share).
- group_7 and group_3 will be the low_target_share.

```
data_country_2$country_rec=
  ifelse(data_country_2$country_rec %in%
           c("group_4", "group_5", "group_9"),
         "low_likelihood",
         data_country_2$country_rec
         )
```

```
data_country_2$country_rec=
  ifelse(data_country_2$country_rec %in%
           c("group_7", "group_3"),
         "low_target_share",
         data_country_2$country_rec
         )
```

Checking the final grouping (country_rec variable):

```
categ_analysis(data = data_country_2,
  input = "country_rec", target = "has_flu")
```

```
##           country_rec mean_target sum_target perc_target
## 1              group_8       0.176         19       0.229
## 2              group_6       0.156         10       0.120
## 3              group_2       0.142         41       0.494
## 4              group_1       0.111         10       0.120
## 5 low_target_share       0.018          3       0.036
## 6   low_likelihood       0.000          0       0.000
##   q_rows perc_rows
```

```
## 1      108      0.119
## 2       64      0.070
## 3      288      0.316
## 4       90      0.099
## 5      169      0.186
## 6      191      0.210
```

Each group seems to have a good sample size regarding the `sum_target` distribution. Our transformation left `low_likelihood` with a representation of 21% of total cases, still with 0 positive cases (`sum_target`=0). And `low_target_share` with 3 positive cases, which represents 3.36% of positive cases.

All the groups seems to have a good representation. This can be checked in `perc_rows` variable. All cases are above of 7% share.

Trying a lower number of cluster may help to reduce this manual task a little. It was just a demonstration of how to optimize a variable having lots of different categories.

2.3.5   Handling new categories when the predictive model is on production

Let's imagine a new country appears, `new_country_hello_world`, predictive models will fail since they were trained with fixed values. One technique is to assign a group which has `mean_target=0`.

It's similar to the case in last example. But the difference lies in `group_5`, this category would fit better in a mid-likelihood group than a complete new value.

After some time we should re-build the model with all new values, otherwise we would be penalizing `new_country_hello_world` if it has a good likelihood.

In so many words:

A new category appears? Send to the least meaningful group. After a while, re-analyze its impact. Does it have a mid or high likelihood? Change it to the most suitable group.

2.3.6 Do predictive models handle high cardinality? Part 1

Yes, and no. Some models deal with this high cardinality issue better than others. In some scenarios, this data preparation may not be necessary. This book tries to expose this issue, which sometimes, may lead to a better model.

Now, we're going throught this by building two predictive models: Gradient Boosting Machine -quite robust across many different data inputs.

The first model doesn't have treated data, and the second one has been treated by the function in `funModeling` package.

We're measuring the precision based on ROC area, ranged from 0.5 to 1, the higher the number the better the model is. We are going to use cross-validation to be *sure* about the value. The importance of cross-validate results is treated in Knowing the error chapter.

```
# Building the first model, without reducing cardinality.
library(caret)
fitControl <- trainControl(method = "cv", number = 4,
  classProbs = TRUE, summaryFunction = twoClassSummary)


fit_gbm_1 <- train(has_flu ~ country,
  data = data_country_2, method = "gbm",
```

```
    trControl = fitControl, verbose = FALSE,
    metric = "ROC")
```

```
# Getting best ROC value
roc = round(max(fit_gbm_1$results$ROC), 2)
```

Area under ROC curve is (**roc**): 0.65.

Now we do the same model with the same parameters, but with the data preparation we did before.

```
# Building the second model, based on the country_rec
# variable
fit_gbm_2 <- train(has_flu ~ country_rec,
    data = data_country_2, method = "gbm",
    trControl = fitControl, verbose = FALSE,
    metric = "ROC")
```

```
# Getting new best ROC value
new_roc = round(max(fit_gbm_2$results$ROC), 2)
```

New ROC curve is (**new_roc**): 0.71.

Then we calculate the percentage of improvement over first roc value:

Improvement: ~ 9.23%. ✅

Not too bad, right?

A short comment about last test:

We've used one of the most robust models, **gradient boosting machine**, and we've increased the performance. If we try other model, for example logistic regression[29], which is more sensible to dirty data, we'll

---

[29]https://en.wikipedia.org/wiki/Logistic_regression

get a higher difference between reducing and not reducing cardinality. This can be checked deleting `verbose=FALSE` parameter and changing `method=glm` (`glm` implies logistic regression).

In *further reading* there is a benchmark of different treatments for categorical variables and how each one increases or decreases the accuracy.

2.3.7 Don't predictive models handle high cardinality? Part 2

Let's review how some models deal with this:

Decision Trees: Tend to select variables with high cardinality at the top, thus giving more importance above others, based on the information gain. In practise, it is evidence of overfitting. This model is good to see the difference between reducing or not a high cardinality variable.

Random Forest -at least in R implementation- handles only categorical variables with at least 52 different categories. It's highly probable that this limitation is to avoid overfitting. This point in conjunction to the nature of the algorithm -creates lots of trees- reduces the effect of a single decision tree when choosing a high cardinality variable.

Gradient Boosting Machine and **Logistic Regression** converts internally categorical variables into flag or dummy variables. In the example we saw about countries, it implies the -internal- creation of 70 flag variables (this is how `caret` handles formula, if we want to keep the original variable without the dummies, we have to not use a formula). Checking the model we created before:

```
# Checking the first model...
fit_gbm_1$finalModel
```

```
## A gradient boosted model with bernoulli loss function.
## 50 iterations were performed.
## There were 69 predictors of which 8 had non-zero influence.
```

That is: 69 input variables are representing the countries, but the flag columns were reported as not being relevant to make the prediction.

This is related to **Feature engineering**. Also, it's related to Selecting best variables. It is a highly recommended practise to first select those variables which carry the most information, and then create the predictive model.

Conclusion: reducing the cardinality will reduce the quantity of variables in these models.

2.3.8 Numerical or multi-nominal target variable

The book covered only the target as a binary variable, it is planned in the future to cover numerical and multi-value target.

However, if you read up to here, you may want explore on your own having the same idea in mind. In numerical variables, for example forecasting `page visits` on a web site, there will be certain categories of the input variable that which will be more related with a high value on visits, while there are others that are more correlated with low values.

The same goes for multi-nominal output variable, there will be some categories more related to certain values. For example predicting the epidemic degree: `high`, `mid` or `low` based on the city. There will be some cities that correlated more correlated with a high epidemic level than others.

2.3.9 What we've got as an "extra-🦷" from the grouping?

Knowing how categories fell into groups give us information that -in some cases- is good to report. Each category between the group will share similar behavior -in terms of representativeness and prediction power-.

If `Argentina` and `Chile` are in `group_1`, then they are the same, and this is how the model will *see* it.

2.3.10 Representativeness or sample size

This concept is on the analysis of any categorical variable, but it's a very common topic in data science and statistics: **sample size**[30]. How much data is it needed to see the pattern *well developed?*.

In a categorical variable: How many cases of category "X" do we need to trust in the correlation between "X" value and a target value? This is what we've analyzed.

In general terms: the more difficult the event to predict, the more cases we need. . .

Further in this book we'll cover this topic from other points of view linking back to this page.

2.3.11 Final thoughts

- We saw two cases to reduce cardinality, the first one doesn't care about the target variable, which can be dangerous in a predictive model, while the second one does. It creates a new variable based on the affinity -and representativity- of each input category to the target variable.

---

[30]https://en.wikipedia.org/wiki/Sample_size_determination

- Key concept: **representativeness** of each category regarding itself, and regarding to the event being predicted. One good point to explore is to analyze it based on statistical tests.

- What was mentioned in the beginning in respects to **destroying the information in the input variable**, implies that the resultant grouping have the same rates across groups (in a binary variable input).

- *Should we always reduce the cardinality?* It depends, two tests on a simple data are not enough to extrapolate all cases. Hopefully it will be a good kick-off for the reader to start doing her-his own optimizations when they consider relevant for the project.

2.3.12 Further reading

- Following link contains many different accuracy results based on different treatments for categorical variable: Beyond One-Hot: an exploration of categorical variables[31].

---

[31] http : / / www . kdnuggets . com / 2015 / 12 / beyond - one - hot - exploration - categorical- variables.html

2.4 Treatment of outliers

2.4.1 What is this about?

The concept of extreme values, much like other topics in machine learning, is not a concept exclusive to this area. What it is an outlier today may not be tomorrow. The boundaries between normal and abnormal behavior are fuzzy; on the other hand, to stand in the extremes is easy.

– When the abnormal is just a matter of perspective –

DATA SCIENCE LIVE BOOK

Image created by: Guillermo Mesyngier[32]

What are we going to review in this chapter?

- What is an outlier? Philosophical and practical approaches
- Outliers by dimensionality and data type (numerical or categorical)
- How to detect outliers in R (bottom/top X%, Tukey and Hampel)
- Outliers preparation for profiling in R
- Outliers preparation for predictive modeling in R

---

[32]https://dribbble.com/gmesyngier

2.4.2 The intuition behind outliers

For example, consider the following distribution:

```
# Loading ggplot2 to visualize the distribution
library(ggplot2)

# Creating a sample dataset
set.seed(31415)
df_1 = data.frame(var = round(10000 * rbeta(1000, 0.15,
  2.5)))

# Plotting
ggplot(df_1, aes(var, fill = var)) +
  geom_histogram(bins = 20) + theme_light()
```

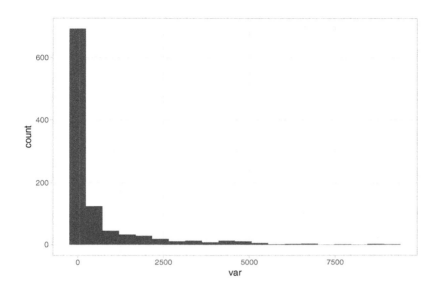

Figure 36: Sample distribution with long tail

The variable is skewed to the left, showing some outlier points on the right. We want to *deal with them* (😎). So, the question arises: *Where to set the thresholds of extreme?* Based on intuition, it can be at the highest 1%, or we can analyze the mean change after removing the top 1%.

Both cases could be right. In fact, taking another number as the threshold (i.e., 2% or 0.1%), may be right too. Let's visualize them:

```
# Calculating the percentiles for the top 3% and top 1%
percentile_var = quantile(df_1$var, c(0.98, 0.99,
  0.999), na.rm = T)
df_p = data.frame(value = percentile_var,
  percentile = c("a_98th", "b_99th", "c_99.9th"))
```

```
# Plotting the same distribution plus the percentiles
ggplot(df_1, aes(var)) + geom_histogram(bins = 20) +
  geom_vline(data = df_p, aes(xintercept = value,
    colour = percentile), show.legend = TRUE,
    linetype = "dashed") + theme_light()
```

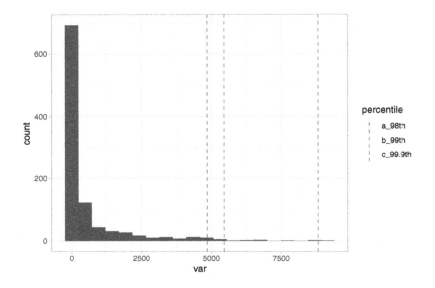

Figure 37: Different thresholds for outliers

To understand more about percentiles, please go to the Annex 1: The magic of percentiles chapter.

For now, we'll keep with the top 1% (99th percentile), as the threshold to flag all the points after it as outliers.

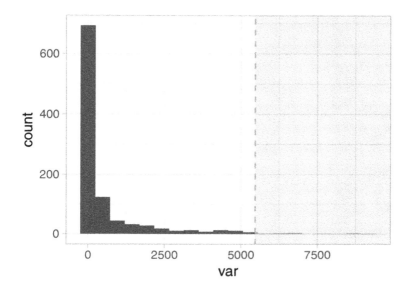

Figure 38: Flagging top 1 percent as outlier

One interesting conceptual element arises here: when we define **abnormal** (or an anomaly), the **normal concept emerges as its opposite**.

This "normal" behavior is shown as the green area:

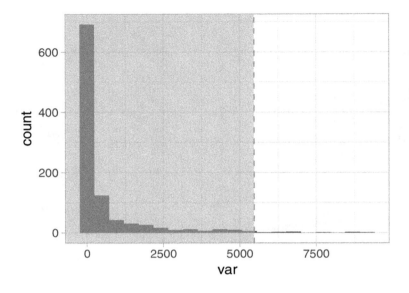

Figure 39: Same threshold, different perspective

The hard thing to do is to determine where the normal and abnormal separate. There are several approaches to deal with this. We are going to review a few of them.

2.4.3 Where is the boundary between hot and cold weather?

Let's make this section more philosophical. Some good mathematicians were also philosophers such as the case of Pythagoras[33] and Isaac Newton[34].

---

[33] https://en.wikipedia.org/wiki/Pythagoras
[34] https://en.wikipedia.org/wiki/Isaac_Newton

Where can we put the threshold to indicate where the hot weather begins or, conversely, where does the cold weather end?

Figure 40: Where is the cutpoint?

Near the Equator, probably a temperature around 10°C (50°F) is an extremely low value; however, in Antarctica, it's a beach day! ☃ 🐊

🦋: *"Oh! But that is taking an extreme example with two different locations!"*

No problem! Like a fractal, let's zoom into any city, the boundary when one starts (and the other ends) will not have one unique value to state the following: *"Ok, the hot weather starts at 25.5°C (78°F)."*

It's relative.

However, it's quite easy to stand in the extremes, where the uncertainty decreases to almost zero, for example, when we consider a temperature of 60°C (140°F).

🌚: *"Ok. But how are these concepts related to machine learning?"*

We're exposing here the relativity that exists when considering a label (hot/cold) as a numeric variable (temperature). This can be considered for any other numeric, such as income and the labels "normal" and "abnormal."

To understand **extreme values** is one of the first tasks in **exploratory data analysis**. Then we can see what the normal values are. This is covered in the Profiling chapter.

There are several methods to flag values as outliers. Just as we might analyze the temperature, this flag is *relative* and all the methods can be right. The quickest method may be to treat the top and bottom X% as outliers.

More robust methods consider the distribution variables by using quantiles (Tukey's method) or the spread of the values through standard deviation (Hampel's method).

The definition of these boundaries is one of the most common tasks in machine learning. *Why? When?* Let's point out two examples:

- Example 1: When we develop a predictive model which returns a probabilty for calling or not certain client, we need to set the score threshold to assign the final label: "yes call!"/"no call". More info about it in Scoring data chapter.

- Example 2: Another example is when we need to discretize a numerical variable because we need it as categorical. The boundaries in each bin/segment will affect the overall result. More info about it in the Discretizing numerical variables section.

✘Going back to the original issue (*where does the cold weather end?*), not all the questions need to have an answer: some of them just help us simply to think.

2.4.4 The impact of outliers

2.4.4.1 Model building

Some models, such as random forest and gradient-boosting machines, tend to deal better with outliers; however, "noise" may affect the results anyway. The impact of outliers in these models is lower than others,

138

such as linear regressions, logistic regressions, kmeans, and decision trees.

One aspect that contributes to the decrease in impact is that both models create *many* sub-models. If any of the models takes one outlier as information, then other sub-models probably won't; thus, the error is canceled. The balance yields in the plurality of voices.

2.4.4.2 Communicating results

If we need to report the variables used in the model, we'll end up removing outliers not to see a histogram with only one bar and/or show a biased mean.

It's better to show a nonbiased number than justifying that the model *will handle* extreme values.

2.4.4.3 Types of outliers by data type

- **Numerical** : Like the one we saw before:

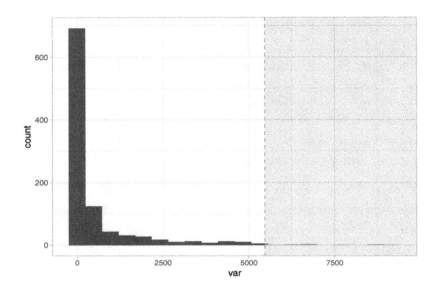

Figure 41: Numerical variable with outliers

- **Categorical** 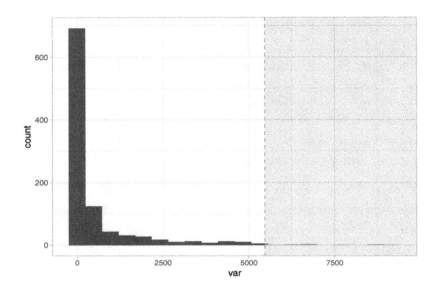: Having a variable in which the dispersion of categories is quite high (high cardinality): for example, postal code. More about dealing with outliers in categorical variables in the High Cardinality Variable in Descriptive Stats chapter.

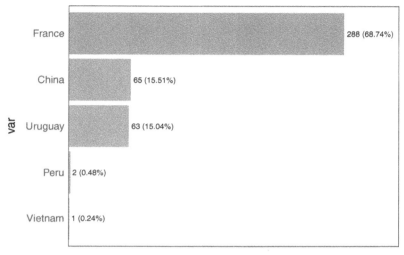

France 288 (68.74%)

China 65 (15.51%)

var Uruguay 63 (15.04%)

Peru 2 (0.48%)

Vietnam 1 (0.24%)

Frequency / (Percentage %)

Figure 42: Categorical variable with outliers

```
##         var frequency percentage cumulative_perc
## 1  France       288      68.74           68.74
## 2   China        65      15.51           84.25
## 3 Uruguay        63      15.04           99.29
## 4    Peru         2       0.48           99.77
## 5 Vietnam         1       0.24          100.00
```

Peru and Vietnam are the outlier countries in this example as their share in the data is less than 1%.

2.4.4.4 Types of outliers by dimensionality

So far, we have observed one-dimensional univariate outliers. We also can consider two or more variables at a time.

141

For instance, we have the following dataset, `df_hello_world`, with two variables: v1 and v2. Doing the same analysis as before:

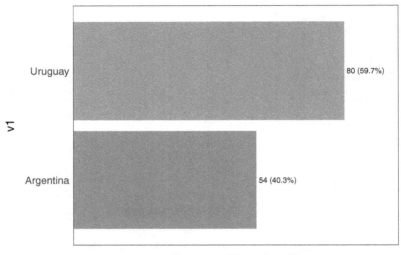

Figure 43: Outliers by dimensionality

```
##            v1 frequency percentage cumulative_perc
## 1   Uruguay        80       59.7            59.7
## 2 Argentina        54       40.3           100.0
```

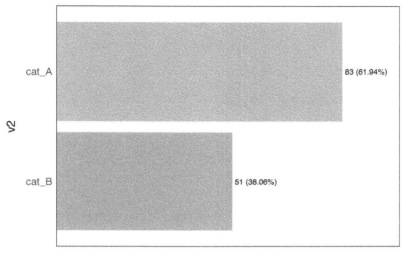

cat_A   83 (61.94%)

cat_B   51 (38.06%)

v2

Frequency / (Percentage %)

Figure 44: Outliers by dimensionality

```
##        v2 frequency percentage cumulative_perc
## 1 cat_A        83       61.94           61.94
## 2 cat_B        51       38.06          100.00

## [1] "Variables processed: v1, v2"
```

No outlier so far, right?

Now we build a contingency table that tells us the distribution of both variables against each other:

```
##                 v2
## v1          cat_A cat_B
##    Argentina 39.55  0.75
##    Uruguay   22.39 37.31
```

Oh 😱! The combination of **Argentina** and **cat_B** is *really low* (0.75%)

in comparison with the other values (less than 1%), whereas the other intersections are above 22%.

2.4.4.5 Some thoughts...

The last examples show the *potential* of extreme values or outliers and are presented as considerations we must make with a new dataset.

We mention **1%** as a possible threshold to flag a value as an outlier. This value could be 0.5% or 3%, depending on the case.

In addition, the presence of this kind of outlier may not pose a problem.

2.4.5 How to deal with outliers in R

The `prep_outliers` function present in the funModeling package can help us in this task. It can handle from one to 'N' variables at a time (by specifying the `input` parameter).

The core is as follows:

- It supports three different methods (`method` parameter) to consider a value as an outlier: bottom_top, Tukey, and Hampel.
- It works in two modes (`type` parameter) by setting an `NA` value or by *stopping the variable* at a particular value. Besides the explanation below, `prep_outliers` is a well-documented function: `help("prep_outliers")`.

2.4.6 Step 1: How to detect outliers 🔎

The following methods are implemented in the `prep_outliers` function. They retrieve different results so the user can select the one that best fits her or his needs.

2.4.6.0.1 Bottom and top values method

This considers outliers based on the bottom and top X% values, based on the percentile. The values are commonly 0.5%, 1%, 1.5%, 3%, among others.

Setting the parameter `top_percent` in `0.01` will treat all values in the top 1%.

The same logic applies for the lowest values: setting the parameter `bottom_percent` to `0.01` will flag as outliers the lowest 1% of all values.

The internal function used is `quantile`; if we want to flag bottom and top 1%, we type:

```
quantile(heart_disease$age, probs = c(0.01, 0.99),
  na.rm = T)
```

```
##  1% 99%
##  35  71
```

All values for those aged less than 35 or more than 71 years will be considered outliers.

For more information about percentiles, check the chapter: The magic of percentiles.

2.4.6.0.2 Tukey's method

This method flags outliers considering the quartiles values, Q1, Q2, and Q3, where Q1 is equivalent to the percentile 25th, Q2 equals to percentile 50th (also known as the median), and Q3 is the percentile 75th.

The IQR (Inter-quartile range) comes from Q3 - Q1.

145

The formula:

- The bottom threshold is: Q1 - 3*IQR. All below are considered as outliers.
- The top threshold is: Q1 + 3*IQR. All above are considered as outliers.

The value 3 is to consider the "extreme" boundary detection. This method comes from the box plot, where the multiplier is 1.5 (not 3). This causes a lot more values to be flagged as shown in the next image.

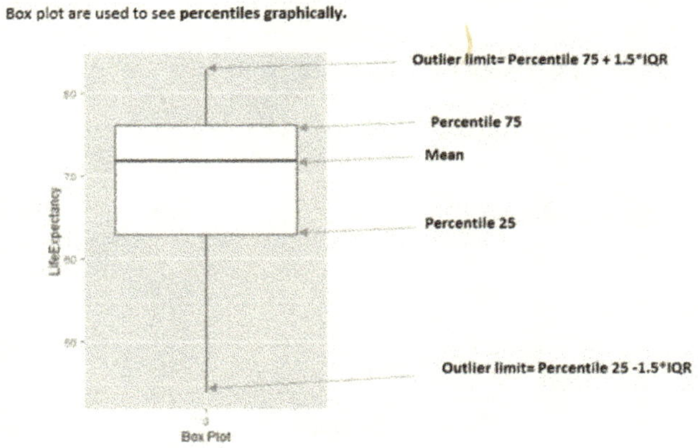

Figure 45: How to interpret a boxplot

The internal function used in `prep_outliers` to calculate the Tukey's boundary can be accessed:

```
tukey_outlier(heart_disease$age)
```

```
## bottom_threshold    top_threshold
##                 9              100
```

It returns a two-value vector; thus, we have the bottom and the top thresholds: all below nine and all above 100 will be considered as outliers.

A subtle visual and step-by-step example can be found in [tukey_outliers].

2.4.6.0.3 Hampel's method

The formula:

- The bottom threshold is: `median_value - 3*mad_value`. All below are considered as outliers.
- The top threshold is: `median_value + 3*mad_value`. All above are considered as outliers.

The internal function used in **prep_outliers** to calculate the Hampel's boundary can be accessed:

```
hampel_outlier(heart_disease$age)
```

```
## bottom_threshold      top_threshold
##            29.3132          82.6868
```

It returns a two-value vector; thus, we have the bottom and the top thresholds. All below 29.31 and all above 82.68 will be considered as outliers.

It has one parameter named `k_mad_value`, and its default value is 3. The value `k_mad_value` can be changed, but not in the **prep_outliers** function by now.

The higher the `k_mad_value`, the higher the threshold boundaries will be.

```
hampel_outlier(heart_disease$age, k_mad_value = 6)
```

```
## bottom_threshold      top_threshold
##             2.6264         109.3736
```

2.4.7 Step 2: What to do with the outliers?

We've already detected which points are the outliers. Therefore, the question now is: *What to do with them?*

There are two scenarios:

- Scenario 1: Prepare outliers for data profiling
- Scenario 2: Prepare outliers for predictive modeling

There is a third scenario in which we don't do anything with the spotted outliers. We just let them be.

We propose the function `prep_outliers` from the `funModeling` package to give a hand on this task.

Regardless the function itself, the important point here is the underlying concept and the possibility of developing an improved method.

The `prep_outliers` function covers these two scenarios through the parameter `type`:

- `type = "set_na"`, for scenario 1
- `type = "stop"`, for scenario 2

2.4.7.1 Scenario 1: Prepare outliers for data profiling

The initial analysis:

In this case, all outliers are converted into `NA`, thus applying most of the characteristic functions (max, min, mean, etc.) will return a **less-biased indicator** value. Remember to set the `na.rm=TRUE` parameter in those functions. Otherwise, the result will be `NA`.

148

For example, let's consider the following variable (the one we saw at the beginning with some outliers):

```
# To understand all of these metrics, please go to the
# Profiling Data chapter
profiling_num(df_1$var)
```

```
##    variable mean std_dev variation_coef p_01 p_05 p_25
## 1       var  548    1226            2.2    0    0    0
##    p_50 p_75 p_95 p_99 skewness kurtosis iqr
## 1    24  370 3382 5467      3.3       16 370
##         range_98      range_80
## 1  [0, 5467.33]  [0, 1791.1]
```

Here we can see several indicators that give us some clues. The `std_dev` is really high compared with the `mean`, and it is reflected on the `variation_coef`. In addition, the kurtosis is high (16) and the `p_99` is almost twice the `p_95` value (5767 vs. 3382).

This last task of looking at some numbers and visualize the variable distribution is like imaging a picture by what another person tells us: we convert the voice (which is a signal) into an image in our brain.
🗣👀 ... => ⛰

2.4.7.1.1 Using `prep_outliers` for data profiling

We need to set `type="set_na"`. This implies that every point flagged as an outlier will be converted into `NA`.

We will use the three methods: Tukey, Hampel, and the bottom/top X%.

Using Tukey's method:

```
df_1$var_tukey = prep_outliers(df_1$var,
  type = "set_na", method = "tukey")
```

Now, we check how many NA values are there before (the original variable) and after the transformation based on Tukey.

```
# before
df_status(df_1$var, print_results = F) %>%
  select(variable, q_na, p_na)
```

```
##     variable q_na p_na
## 1        var    0    0
```

```
# after
df_status(df_1$var_tukey, print_results = F) %>%
  select(variable, q_na, p_na)
```

```
##     variable q_na p_na
## 1        var  120   12
```

Before the transformation, there were 0 NA values, whereas afterwards 120 values (around 12%) are spotted as outliers according to the Tukey's test and replaced by NA.

We can compare the before and after:

```
profiling_num(df_1, print_results = F) %>%
  select(variable, mean, std_dev, variation_coef,
    kurtosis, range_98)
```

```
##      variable mean std_dev variation_coef kurtosis
## 1         var  548    1226            2.2     15.6
## 2 var_tukey   163     307            1.9      8.4
##          range_98
## 1 [0, 5467.33]
## 2 [0, 1358.46]
```

The mean decreased by almost the third part while all the other metrics decreased as well.

Hampel's method:

Let's see what happens with Hampel's method (`method="hampel"`):

```
df_1$var_hampel = prep_outliers(df_1$var,
  type = "set_na", method = "hampel")
```

Checking...

```
df_status(df_1, print_results = F) %>% select(variable,
  q_na, p_na)
```

```
##      variable q_na p_na
## 1         var    0    0
## 2   var_tukey  120   12
## 3  var_hampel  364   36
```

This last method is much more severe in spotting outliers, identifying 36% of values as outliers. This is probably because the variable is *quite* skewed to the left.

Bottom and top X% method

Finally, we can try the easiest method: to remove the top 2%.

```
df_1$var_top2 = prep_outliers(df_1$var, type = "set_na",
  method = "bottom_top", top_percent = 0.02)
```

Please note that the 2% value was arbitrarily chosen. Other values, like 3% or 0.5%, can be tried as well.

Time to compare all the methods!

2.4.7.1.2 Putting it all together

We'll pick a few indicators to make the quantitative comparison.

```r
df_status(df_1, print_results = F) %>% select(variable,
  q_na, p_na)
```

```
##       variable q_na p_na
## 1         var    0    0
## 2   var_tukey  120   12
## 3 var_hampel  364   36
## 4    var_top2   20    2
```

```r
prof_num = profiling_num(df_1, print_results = F) %>%
  select(variable, mean, std_dev, variation_coef,
    kurtosis, range_98)
prof_num
```

```
##       variable mean std_dev variation_coef kurtosis
## 1         var  548    1226            2.2     15.6
## 2   var_tukey  163     307            1.9      8.4
## 3 var_hampel   17      31            1.8      6.0
## 4    var_top2  432     908            2.1     10.9
##          range_98
## 1 [0, 5467.33]
## 2 [0, 1358.46]
## 3   [0, 118.3]
## 4 [0, 4364.29]
```

Plotting

```r
# First we need to convert the dataset into wide format
df_1_m = reshape2::melt(df_1)
plotar(df_1_m, target = "variable", input = "value",
  plot_type = "boxplot")
```

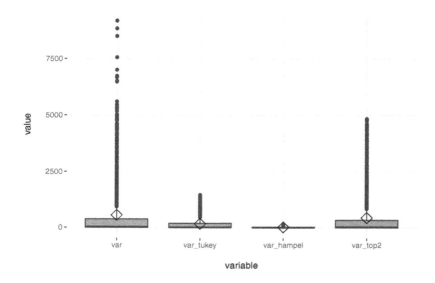

Figure 46: Outliers methods comparison

When selecting the bottom/top X%, we will always have some values matching that condition, whereas with other methods this may not be the case.

2.4.7.1.3 Conclusions for dealing with outliers in data profiling

The idea is to modify the outliers as least as possible (for example, if we were interested only in describing the general behavior).

To accomplish this task, for example when creating an ad hoc report, we can use the mean. We could choose the top 2% method because it only affects 2% of all values and causes the mean to be lowered drastically: from 548 to 432, or **21% less**.

"To modify or not to modify the dataset, that is the question". William Shakespeare being a Data Scientist.

The Hampel method modified the mean too much, from 548 to 17! That is based on the *standard* value considered with this method, which is 3-MAD (kind of robust standard deviation).

Please note that this demonstration doesn't mean that neither Hampel nor Tukey are a bad choice. In fact, they are more robust because the threshold can be higher than the current value; indeed, no value is treated as an outlier.

On the other extreme, we can consider, for example, the `age` variable from `heart_disease` data. Let's analyze its outliers:

```
# Getting outliers threshold
tukey_outlier(heart_disease$age)
```

```
## bottom_threshold    top_threshold
##                9              100
```

```
# Getting min and max values
min(heart_disease$age)
```

```
## [1] 29
```

```
max(heart_disease$age)
```

```
## [1] 77
```

- The bottom threshold is 9, and the minimum value is 29.
- The top threshold is 100, and the maximum value is 77.

Ergo: the `age` variable has not outliers.

If we were to have used the bottom/top method, then the input percentages would have been detected as outliers.

All the examples so far have been taking one variable at a time;

however, `prep_outliers` can handle several at the same time using the parameter `input` as we will see in next section. All that we have seen up to here will be equivalent, except for what we do once we detect the outlier, i.e., the imputation method.

2.4.7.2 Scenario 2: Prepare outliers for predictive modeling

The previous case results in spotted outliers being converted to `NA` values. This is a huge problem if we are building a machine learning model as many of them don't work with `NA` values. More about dealing with missing data at Analysis, Handling, and Imputation of Missing Data.

To deal with outliers in order to use a predictive model, we can adjust the parameter `type='stop'` so all values flagged as outliers will be converted to the threshold value.

Some things to keep in mind:

Try to think of variable treatment (and creation) as if you're explaining to the model. By stopping variables at a certain value, 1% for example, we are telling to the model: *Hey model, please consider all extreme values as if they are in the 99% percentile as this value is already high enough. Thanks.*

Some predictive models are more **noise tolerant** than others. We can help them by treating some of the outlier values. In practice, to pre-process data by treating outliers tends to produce more accurate results in the presence of unseen data.

2.4.7.3 Imputing outliers for predictive modeling

First, we create a dataset with some outliers. Now the example has two variables.

```
# Creating data frame with outliers

# deactivating scientific notation
options(scipen = 999)
# setting the seed to have a reproducible example
set.seed(10)
# creating the variables
df_2 = data.frame(var1 = rchisq(1000, df = 1),
  var2 = rnorm(1000))
# forcing outliers
df_2 = rbind(df_2, 135, rep(400, 30), 245, 300, 303,
  200)
```

Dealing with outliers in both variables (var1 and var2) using Tukey's method:

```
df_2_tukey = prep_outliers(data = df_2,
  input = c("var1", "var2"), type = "stop",
  method = "tukey")
```

Checking some metrics before and after the imputation:

```
profiling_num(df_2, print_results = F) %>%
  select(variable, mean, std_dev, variation_coef)

##    variable mean std_dev variation_coef
## 1      var1  2.6      21            8.3
## 2      var2  1.6      21           13.6

profiling_num(df_2_tukey, print_results = F) %>%
  select(variable, mean, std_dev, variation_coef)

##    variable  mean std_dev variation_coef
## 1      var1 0.997     1.3            1.3
## 2      var2 0.018     1.0           57.5
```

Tukey worked perfectly this time, exposing a more accurate mean in both variables: 1 for var1 and 0 for var2.

Note that this time there is no one NA value. What the function did this time was **"to stop the variable"** at the threshold values. Now, the minimum and maximum values will be the same as the ones reported by Tukey's method.

Checking the threshold for var1:

```
tukey_outlier(df_2$var1)
```

```
## bottom_threshold     top_threshold
##              -3.8               5.3
```

Now checking the min/max before the transformation:

```
# before:
min(df_2$var1)
```

```
## [1] 0.0000031
```

```
max(df_2$var1)
```

```
## [1] 400
```

and after the transformation...

```
# after
min(df_2_tukey$var1)
```

```
## [1] 0.0000031
```

```
max(df_2_tukey$var1)
```

```
## [1] 5.3
```

The min remains the same (0.0000031), but the maximum was set to the Tukey's value of ~5.3.

The top five highest values before the pre-partition were:

```
# before
tail(df_2$var1[order(df_2$var1)], 5)
```

```
## [1] 200 245 300 303 400
```

but after...

```
# after:
tail(df_2_tukey$var1[order(df_2_tukey$var1)], 5)
```

```
## [1] 5.3 5.3 5.3 5.3 5.3
```

And checking there is no one NA:

```
df_status(df_2_tukey, print_results = F) %>%
  select(variable, q_na, p_na)
```

```
##    variable q_na p_na
## 1     var1    0    0
## 2     var2    0    0
```

Pretty clear, right?

Now let's replicate the example we did in the last section with only one variable in order to compare all three methods.

```
df_2$tukey_var2 = prep_outliers(data = df_2$var2,
  type = "stop", method = "tukey")
df_2$hampel_var2 = prep_outliers(data = df_2$var2,
  type = "stop", method = "hampel")
df_2$bot_top_var2 = prep_outliers(data = df_2$var2,
  type = "stop", method = "bottom_top",
  bottom_percent = 0.01, top_percent = 0.01)
```

2.4.7.3.1 Putting it all together

```r
# excluding var1
df_2_b = select(df_2, -var1)

# profiling
profiling_num(df_2_b, print_results = F) %>%
  select(variable, mean, std_dev, variation_coef,
    kurtosis, range_98)
```

```
##          variable    mean std_dev variation_coef kurtosis
## 1            var2 1.5649   21.36              14    223.8
## 2      tukey_var2 0.0178    1.02              58      4.6
## 3     hampel_var2 0.0083    0.98             118      3.2
## 4   bot_top_var2 0.0083    0.97             116      2.9
##          range_98
## 1  [-2.32, 2.4]
## 2  [-2.32, 2.4]
## 3  [-2.32, 2.4]
## 4  [-2.32, 2.4]
```

All three methods show very similar results with these data.

Plotting

```r
# First we need to convert the dataset into wide format
df_2_m = reshape2::melt(df_2_b) %>% filter(value < 100)
plotar(df_2_m, target = "variable", input = "value",
  plot_type = "boxplot")
```

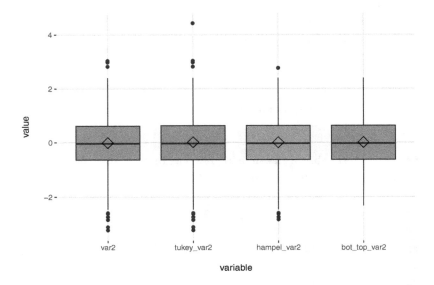

Figure 47: Comparing outliers methods

Important: The two points above the value 100 (only for **var1**) were excluded, otherwise it was impossible to appreciate the difference between the methods.

2.4.8   Final thoughts

We've covered the outliers issue from both philosophical and technical perspectives, thereby inviting the reader to improve her/his critical thinking skills when defining the boundaries (thresholds). It is easy to stand in the extremes, but a tough task to find the balance.

In technical terms, we covered three methods to spot outliers whose bases are different:

- **Bottom/Top X%**: This will always detect points as outliers as there is always a bottom and top X%.
- **Tukey**: Based on the classical boxplot, which uses the quartiles.
- **Hampel**: Quite restrictive if default parameter is not changed. It's based on the median and MAD values (similar to standard deviation, but less sensitive to outliers).

After we've got the outliers, the next step is to decide what to do with them. It would be the case that the treatment is not necessary at all. In really small datasets, they can be seen at first glance.

The rule of: *"Only modify what is necessary"*, (which can also apply to the *human being–nature* relationship), tells us not to treat or exclude all the extreme outliers blindly. **With every action we took, we introduced some bias**. That's why it's so important to know the implications of every method. Whether it is a good decision or not is dependent on the nature of the data under analysis.

In **predictive modeling**, those who have any type of internal resampling technique, or create *several tiny models* to get a final prediction, are more stable to extreme values. More on resampling and error in the Knowing the error chapter.

In some cases when the predictive model is **running on production**, it's recommended to report or to consider the preparation of any new extreme value, i.e., a value that was not present during the model building. More on this topic, but with a categorical variable, can be found at High Cardinality Variable in Predictive Modeling, section: *Handling new categories when the predictive model is on production*.

One nice test for the reader to do is to pick up a dataset, treat the outliers, and then compare some performance metrics like Kappa, ROC, Accuracy, etc.; **did the data preparation improve any of them?** Or, in reporting, to see how much the mean changes. Even if we plot some variable, does the plot now tell us anything?. In this way, the reader will create new knowledge based on her/his experience .

Data Science Live Book

2.5 Missing Data: Analysis, Handling, and Imputation of

2.5.1 What is this about?

The analysis of missing values is the estimation of emptiness itself. Missing values present an obstacle to creating predictive models, cluster analyses, reports, etc.

In this chapter, we discuss the concept and treatment of empty values. We will perform analyses using different approaches and interpret the different results.

Hopefully, after studying the whole chapter, the reader will understand key concepts of dealing with missing values and pursue better approaches than the ones proposed here.

What are we going to review in this chapter?

- What is the concept of an empty value?
- When to exclude rows or columns.
- Analysis and profiling of missing values.
- Transforming and imputing numeric and categorical variables.
- Imputing values: from easy to more complex approaches.

These will be exemplified using a practical approach in R. The code intends to be generic enough to apply to your projects 😊.

2.5.2 When the empty value represents information

Empty values are also known as "NULL" in databases, NA in R, or just the "empty" string in spreadsheet programs. It can also be represented by some number like: 0, -1 or -999.

For example, imagine a travel agency that joins two tables, one of persons and another of countries. The result shows the number of travels per person:

```
##      person South_Africa Brazil Costa_Rica
## 1   Fotero            1      5          5
## 2    Herno           NA     NA         NA
## 3 Mamarul           34     40         NA
```

In this result, Mamarul traveled to South Africa 34 times.

What does the NA (or NULL) value represent?

In this case, NA should be replaced by 0, indicating zero travels in that person–country intersection. After the conversion, the table is ready to be used.

Example: Replace all NA values by 0

```
# Making a copy
df_travel_2 = df_travel

# Replacing all NA values with 0
df_travel_2[is.na(df_travel_2)] = 0
df_travel_2
```

```
##      person South_Africa Brazil Costa_Rica
## 1  Fotero            1      5          5
## 2   Herno            0      0          0
## 3 Mamarul           34     40          0
```

The last example transforms **all NA** values into 0. However, in other scenarios, this transformation may not apply to all columns.

Example: Replace NA values by 0 only in certain columns

It is probably the most common scenario to replace NA by some value—zero in this case—only to some columns. We define a vector containing all the variables to replace and then we call on the `mutate_at` function from the `dplyr` package.

```
library(dplyr)  # vers 0.7.1

# Replacing NA values with 0 only in selected columns
vars_to_replace = c("Brazil", "Costa_Rica")

df_travel_3 = df_travel %>%
  mutate_at(.vars = vars_to_replace,
    .funs = funs(ifelse(is.na(.),
      0, .)))


df_travel_3
```

```
##      person South_Africa Brazil Costa_Rica
## 1  Fotero            1      5          5
## 2   Herno           NA      0          0
## 3 Mamarul           34     40          0
```

Keep at hand the last function as it is very common to face the situation of applying a specified function to a subset of variables and returning the transformed and the non-transformed variables in the same dataset.

Let's go to a more complex example.

2.5.3   When the empty value is an empty value

Other times, to have an empty value is correct, it's expressing the absence of something. We need to treat them to use the table. Many predictive models don't handle input tables with missing values.

In some cases, a variable is measured *after* a period of time, so we have data from this point on and NA before.

Sometimes there are random cases, like a machine that fails to collect the data or a user who forgot to complete some field in a form, among others.

One important question arises: *What to do?!* 😱

The following recommendations are just that, recommendations. You can try different approaches to discover the best strategy for the data you are analyzing. **There is no "one-size-fits-all"**.

2.5.4   Excluding the entire row

If at least one column has an NA value, then exclude the row.

A fast and easy method, right? It's recommended when the number of rows is *low*. But how low is low? That's up to you. Ten cases in 1,000 of rows *may not* have a huge impact unless those 10 cases are related to the prediction of an anomaly; in this instance, it represents information. We pointed out this issue in Case 1: reducing by re-categorizing less representative values.

Example in R:

Let's inspect the `heart_disease` dataset with the `df_status` function, where one of its primary objectives is to help us with these kinds of decisions.

```
library(dplyr)
library(funModeling)
df_status(heart_disease, print_results = F) %>%
  select(variable, q_na, p_na) %>% arrange(-q_na)
```

```
##                       variable q_na p_na
## 1          num_vessels_flour    4 1.32
## 2                        thal    2 0.66
## 3                         age    0 0.00
## 4                      gender    0 0.00
## 5                  chest_pain    0 0.00
## 6       resting_blood_pressure    0 0.00
## 7             serum_cholestoral    0 0.00
## 8          fasting_blood_sugar    0 0.00
## 9              resting_electro    0 0.00
## 10              max_heart_rate    0 0.00
## 11                 exer_angina    0 0.00
## 12                     oldpeak    0 0.00
## 13                       slope    0 0.00
## 14      heart_disease_severity    0 0.00
## 15                 exter_angina    0 0.00
## 16          has_heart_disease    0 0.00
```

`q_na` indicates the quantity of `NA` values and `p_na` is the percentage. Full info about `df_status` can be found in Profiling chapter.

Two variables have 4 and 2 rows with `NA` values, so we exclude these rows:

```
# na.omit returns the same data frame having excluded all
# rows containing at least one NA value
```

```
heart_disease_clean = na.omit(heart_disease)
nrow(heart_disease)   # number of rows before exclusion
```

[1] 303

```
nrow(heart_disease_clean)   # number of rows after exclusion
```

[1] 297

After the exclusion, six rows out of 303 were eliminated. This approach seems suitable for this dataset.

However, there are other scenarios in which almost all cases are empty values, thus exclusion will delete the entire dataset!

2.5.5   Excluding the column

Similar to the last case, we exclude the column. If we apply the same reasoning and if the deletion is about a *few* columns and the remaining ones provide a reliable final result, then it may be acceptable.

Example in R:

These exclusions are easily handled with the `df_status` function. The following code will keep all variable names for which the percentage of NA values are higher than 0.

```
# Getting variable names with NA values
vars_to_exclude = df_status(heart_disease,
  print_results = F) %>% filter(p_na > 0) %>%
  .$variable

# Checking variables to exclude
vars_to_exclude
```

167

```
## [1] "num_vessels_flour" "thal"
```

```
# Excluding variables from original dataset
heart_disease_clean_2 = select(heart_disease,
  -one_of(vars_to_exclude))
```

2.5.6 Treating empty values in categorical variables

We cover different perspectives to convert as well as treat empty values in nominal variables.

Data for the following example are derived from `web_navigation_data` which contains standard information regarding how users come to a particular web page. It contains the `source_page` (the page the visitor comes from), `landing_page` (first page visited), and `country`.

```
# When reading example data, pay attention to
# the na.strings parameter
web_navigation_data=
  read.delim(file="https://goo.gl/dz7zNx",
             sep="\t",
             header = T,
             stringsAsFactors=F,
             na.strings="")
```

2.5.6.1 Profiling the data

```
stat_nav_data = df_status(web_navigation_data)
```

```
##        variable q_zeros p_zeros q_na p_na q_inf p_inf
## 1   source_page       0       0   50 51.5     0     0
## 2  landing_page       0       0    5  5.2     0     0
## 3       country       0       0    3  3.1     0     0
```

168

```
##          type unique
## 1 character      5
## 2 character      5
## 3 character     18
```

The three variables have empty (NA) values. Almost half of the values in source_page are missing while the other two variables have 5% and 3% NAs.

2.5.6.2   Case A: Convert the empty value into a string

In categorical or nominal variables, the quickest treatment is to convert the empty value into the string unknown. Therefore, the machine learning model will handle the "empty" values as another category. Think about it like a rule: "If variable_X = unknown, then the outcome = yes".

Next, we propose two methods intended to cover typical scenarios.

Example in R:

```
library(tidyr)

# Method 1: Converting just one variable
web_navigation_data_1=web_navigation_data %>%
  mutate(source_page =
           replace_na(source_page,
                     "unknown_source")
        )



# Method 2: It's a typical situation only to apply a
# function to specific variables and then return the
# original data frame
```

```
# Imagine we want to convert all variables with less
# than 6% NA values:
vars_to_process =
  filter(stat_nav_data, p_na<6)[,"variable"]


vars_to_process

## [1] "landing_page" "country"
```

```
# Create the new data frame with the transformed
# variables
web_navigation_data_2=web_navigation_data %>%
  mutate_at(.vars=vars(vars_to_process),
            .funs=funs(replace_na(.,"other"))
            )
```

Checking the results:

```
df_status(web_navigation_data_1)
```

```
##          variable q_zeros p_zeros q_na p_na q_inf p_inf
## 1   source_page       0       0    0  0.0     0     0
## 2 landing_page       0       0    5  5.2     0     0
## 3      country       0       0    3  3.1     0     0
##            type unique
## 1 character      6
## 2 character      5
## 3 character     18
```

```
df_status(web_navigation_data_2)
```

```
##          variable q_zeros p_zeros q_na p_na q_inf p_inf
## 1   source_page       0       0   50   52     0     0
## 2 landing_page       0       0    0    0     0     0
## 3      country       0       0    0    0     0     0
```

```
##         type unique
## 1 character      5
## 2 character      6
## 3 character     19
```

Note: To apply a function to certain columns is a very common task in any data project. More info about how to use it `mutate_at` from `dplyr`: how do I select certain columns and give new names to mutated columns?[35]

2.5.6.3   Case B: Assign the most frequent category

The intuition behind this method is *to add more of the same as to not affect the variable*. However, sometimes it does. It will not have the same impact if the most common value appears 90% of the time than if it does 10%; that is, it depends on the distribution.

There are other scenarios in which we can imput new missing values based on other predictive models just like k-NN. This approach is more suitable than replacing by the most frequent value. However, the recommended technique is the one we seen in *Case A: Convert the empty value into a string*.

2.5.6.4   Case C: Exclude some columns and transform others

The easy case is if the column contains, let's say, 50% `NA` cases, making it highly likely not to be reliable.

In the case we saw before, `source_page` has more than half of the values empty. We could exclude this variable and transform —as we did— the remaining two.

---

[35]https://stackoverflow.com/questions/27027347/mutate-each-summarise-each-in-dplyr-how-do-i-select-certain-columns-and-give

The example is prepared to be generic:

```
# Setting the threshold
threshold_to_exclude = 50   # 50 Represents 50%
vars_to_exclude = filter(stat_nav_data, p_na >=
  threshold_to_exclude)
vars_to_keep = filter(stat_nav_data, p_na <
  threshold_to_exclude)

# Finally...
vars_to_exclude$variable
```

```
## [1] "source_page"
```

```
vars_to_keep$variable
```

```
## [1] "landing_page" "country"
```

```
# Next line will exclude variables above the threshold
# and transform the remaining ones
web_navigation_data_3 = select(web_navigation_data,
  -one_of(vars_to_exclude$variable)) %>%
  mutate_at(.vars = vars(vars_to_keep$variable),
    .funs = funs(replace_na(., "unknown")))


# Checking there are no NA values and the variable above
# the NA threshold has disappeared
df_status(web_navigation_data_3)
```

```
##         variable q_zeros p_zeros q_na p_na q_inf p_inf
## 1 landing_page       0       0    0    0     0     0
## 2      country       0       0    0    0     0     0
##          type unique
## 1 character       6
```

2.5.6.5   Summing-up

What if the data contain 40% `NA` values? It depends on the objective of the analysis and the nature of the data.

The important point here is to "save" the variable so we can use it. Finding many variables with missing values is common. It may be that those *incomplete variables* carry useful predictive information when they have a value, therefore, we need to treat them and then build a predictive model.

However, we need to minimize the bias we are introducing because the missing value is a value that "is not there".

- When doing a report, the suggestion is to replace `NA` by the string `empty`,
- When doing a predictive model that is running live, assign the most repetitive category.

2.5.7   Is there any pattern in missing values?

First, load the example movie data and do a quick profile.

```
# Lock5Data contains many data frames to practice
# install.packages('Lock5Data')
library(Lock5Data)


# loading data
data("HollywoodMovies2011")
```

```
# profiling
df_status(HollywoodMovies2011)

##             variable q_zeros p_zeros q_na  p_na q_inf
## 1             Movie       0    0.00    0  0.00     0
## 2         LeadStudio       0    0.00    0  0.00     0
## 3      RottenTomatoes       0    0.00    2  1.47     0
## 4      AudienceScore       0    0.00    1  0.74     0
## 5             Story        0    0.00    0  0.00     0
## 6             Genre        0    0.00    0  0.00     0
## 7   TheatersOpenWeek       0    0.00   16 11.76     0
## 8  BOAverageOpenWeek       0    0.00   16 11.76     0
## 9      DomesticGross       0    0.00    2  1.47     0
## 10      ForeignGross       0    0.00   15 11.03     0
## 11        WorldGross       0    0.00    2  1.47     0
## 12            Budget       0    0.00    2  1.47     0
## 13     Profitability       1    0.74    2  1.47     0
## 14    OpeningWeekend       1    0.74    3  2.21     0
##    p_inf    type unique
## 1      0  factor    136
## 2      0  factor     34
## 3      0 integer     75
## 4      0 integer     60
## 5      0  factor     22
## 6      0  factor      9
## 7      0 integer    118
## 8      0 integer    120
## 9      0 numeric    130
## 10     0 numeric    121
## 11     0 numeric    134
## 12     0 numeric     60
## 13     0 numeric    134
## 14     0 numeric    130
```

Let's take a look at the values present in the **p_na** column. There is a pattern in the missing values: four variables have 1.47% NA values and another four have around 11.7%. In this case, we are not able to check the data source; however, it is a good idea to check if those cases have a common issue.

2.5.8 Treating missing values in numerical variables

We approached this point at the beginning of the chapter by converting all **NA** values to 0.

One solution is to replace the empty by the mean, median, or other criteria. However, we have to be aware of the change in the distribution that this creates.

If we see that the variable seems to be correlated when it's not empty (same as categorical), the an alternative method is to create bins, also known as "buckets" or "segments", thereby converting it to categorical.

2.5.8.1 Method 1: Converting into categorical

The function **equal_freq** splits the variable into the desired bins. It takes a numeric variable (**TheatersOpenWeek**) and returns a categorical one (**TheatersOpenWeek_cat**), based on equal frequency criteria.

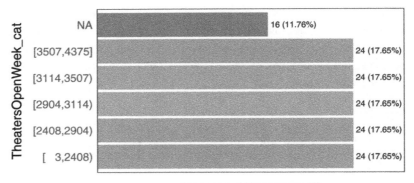

Figure 48: Missing values in categorical data

```
##   TheatersOpenWeek_cat frequency percentage
## 1          [   3,2408)        24         18
## 2          [2408,2904)        24         18
## 3          [2904,3114)        24         18
## 4          [3114,3507)        24         18
## 5          [3507,4375]        24         18
## 6                 <NA>        16         12
##   cumulative_perc
## 1              18
## 2              35
## 3              53
## 4              71
## 5              88
## 6             100
```

As we can see, TheatersOpenWeek_cat contains five buckets of 24 cases each, where each represents ~18% of total cases. But, the NA values are still there.

Finally, we have to convert the NA into the string empty.

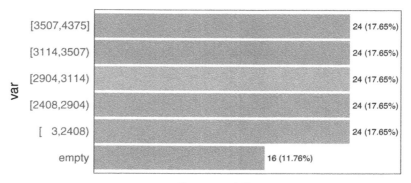

[3507,4375]		24 (17.65%)
[3114,3507)		24 (17.65%)
[2904,3114)		24 (17.65%)
[2408,2904)		24 (17.65%)
[3,2408)		24 (17.65%)
empty		16 (11.76%)

Frequency / (Percentage %)

And that's it: the variable is ready to be used.

Custom cuts:

If we want to use custom bucket sizes instead of the ones provided by equal frequency, then we can use **cut** function. In this case it takes the numerical variable **TheatersOpenWeek** and returns **TheatersOpenWeek_cat_cust**.

```
# disabling scientific notation in current R session
options(scipen=999)


# Creating custom buckets, with limits in 1,000,
# 2,300, and a max of 4,100. Values above 4,100
# will be assigned to NA.


HollywoodMovies2011$TheatersOpenWeek_cat_cust=
  cut(HollywoodMovies2011$TheatersOpenWeek,
      breaks = c(0, 1000, 2300, 4100),
      include.lowest = T,
      dig.lab = 10)


freq(HollywoodMovies2011$TheatersOpenWeek_cat_cust,
```

```
   plot = F)
```

```
##              var frequency  percentage  cumulative_perc
## 1 (2300,4100]        94        69.1                  69
## 2         <NA>       19        14.0                  83
## 3 (1000,2300]        14        10.3                  93
## 4      [0,1000]        9         6.6                 100
```

It should be noted that **equal frequency binning** tends to be more robust than the equal distance that splits the variable, which is based on taking the min and max, and the distance between each segment, regardless how many cases fall into each bucket.

The equal frequency puts the outliers values in the first or last bin as appropriate. Normal values can range from 3 to 20 buckets. A higher number of buckets tend to be noisier. For more info, check the cross_plot chapter function.

2.5.8.2   Method 2: Filling the NA with some value

As with categorical variables, we can replace values by a number such as the mean or the median.

In this case, we'll replace NA by the average and plot the before and after results side-by-side.

```
# Filling all NA values with the mean of the variable
HollywoodMovies2011$TheatersOpenWeek_mean=
  ifelse(is.na(HollywoodMovies2011$TheatersOpenWeek),
       mean(HollywoodMovies2011$TheatersOpenWeek,
          na.rm = T),
       HollywoodMovies2011$TheatersOpenWeek
       )

# Plotting original variable
```

```
p1=ggplot(HollywoodMovies2011, aes(x=TheatersOpenWeek)) +
   geom_histogram(colour="black", fill="white") +
   ylim(0, 30)

# Plotting transformed variable
p2=ggplot(HollywoodMovies2011,
          aes(x=TheatersOpenWeek_mean)
          ) +
   geom_histogram(colour="black", fill="white") +
   ylim(0, 30)

# Putting the plots side-by-side
library(gridExtra)
grid.arrange(p1, p2, ncol=2)
```

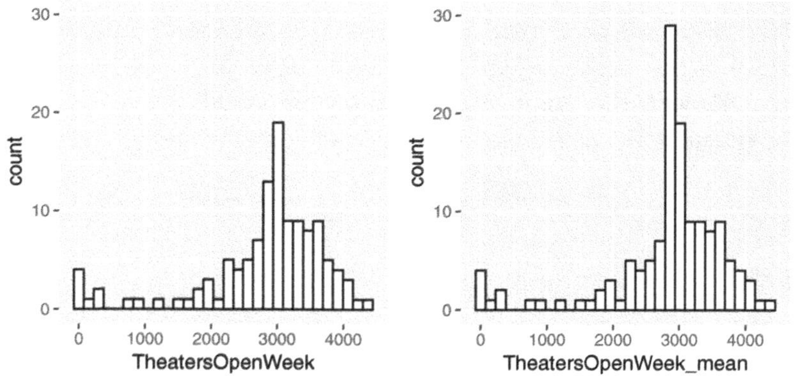

Figure 49: Filling NA with the mean value

We can see a peak at 2828, which is a product of the transformation. This introduces a bias around this point. If we are predicting some event, then it would be safer not to have some special event around

179

this value.

For example, if we are predicting a binary event and the least representative event is correlated with having a mean of 3000 in TheatersOpenWeek, then the odds of having a higher **False Positive rate** may be higher. Again, the link to the High Cardinality Variable in Predictive Modeling chapter.

As an extra comment regarding the last visualization, it was important to set the y-axis maximum to 30 to make the plots comparable.

As you can see, there is an inter-relationship between all concepts 😌.

2.5.8.3 Picking up the right value to fill

The last example replaced the NA with the mean, but how about other values? It depends on the distribution of the variable.

The variable we used (TheatersOpenWeek) seems normally distributed, which is the reason we used the mean. However, if the variable is more skewed, then another metric probably would be more suitable; for example, the median is less sensitive to outliers.

2.5.9 Advanced imputation methods

Now we are going to do a quick review of more sophisticated imputation methods in which we create a predictive model, with all that it implies.

2.5.9.1 Method 1: Using random forest (missForest)

The missForest[36] package its functionality its based on running several random forests in order to complete each missing value in an iterative

---

[36]https://cran.r-project.org/web/packages/missForest/missForest.pdf

process, handling both categorical and numerical variables at the same time.

Regardless of missing value imputation, the random forest model has one of the best performances of many different kinds of data. In next example, we will complete the `HollywoodMovies2011` data we were working with before. These data contain `NA` values in both numerical and categorical variables.

```r
# install.packages("missForest")
library(missForest)

# Copying the data
df_holly=Lock5Data::HollywoodMovies2011

# Creating again the TheatersOpenWeek_cat_cust
df_holly$TheatersOpenWeek_cat_cust=
  cut(HollywoodMovies2011$TheatersOpenWeek,
      breaks = c(0, 1000, 2300, 4100),
      include.lowest = T,
      dig.lab = 10)

# We will introduce 15% more NA values in
# TheatersOpenWeek_3 to produce a better example.
# The function prodNA in missForest will help us.

# seting the seed to get always the same number of
# NA values
set.seed(31415)

df_holly$TheatersOpenWeek_cat_cust=
  prodNA(
    select(df_holly, TheatersOpenWeek_cat_cust),
    0.15
```

```
  )[,1]
```

```r
# Excluding the unuseful variables
df_holly=select(df_holly, -Movie)
```

```r
# Now the magic! Imputing the data frame
# xmis parameter=the data with missing values
imputation_res=missForest(xmis = df_holly)
```

```
##    missForest iteration 1 in progress...done!
##    missForest iteration 2 in progress...done!
##    missForest iteration 3 in progress...done!
##    missForest iteration 4 in progress...done!
```

```r
# Final imputed data frame
df_imputed=imputation_res$ximp
```

Note: **missForest** fails will fail if it has any character variable.

Now it's time to compare the distributions of some of the imputed variables, we will use the original variable before discretization: **TheatersOpenWeek**. Hopefully, they will look similar on a visual analysis.

```r
# Creating another imputation based on na.rougfix from
# the random forest package
df_rough = na.roughfix(df_holly)
```

```r
# Compare distributions before and after imputation
df_holly$imputation = "original"
df_rough$imputation = "na.roughfix"
df_imputed$imputation = "missForest"
```

```r
# Putting the two data frames in only one, but split by
# is_imputed variable
```

182

```
df_all = rbind(df_holly, df_imputed, df_rough)

# Converting to factor for using in a plot
df_all$imputation = factor(df_all$imputation,
  levels = unique(df_all$imputation))

# Plotting
ggplot(df_all, aes(TheatersOpenWeek,
  colour = imputation)) + geom_density() +
  theme_minimal() + scale_colour_brewer(palette = "Set2")
```

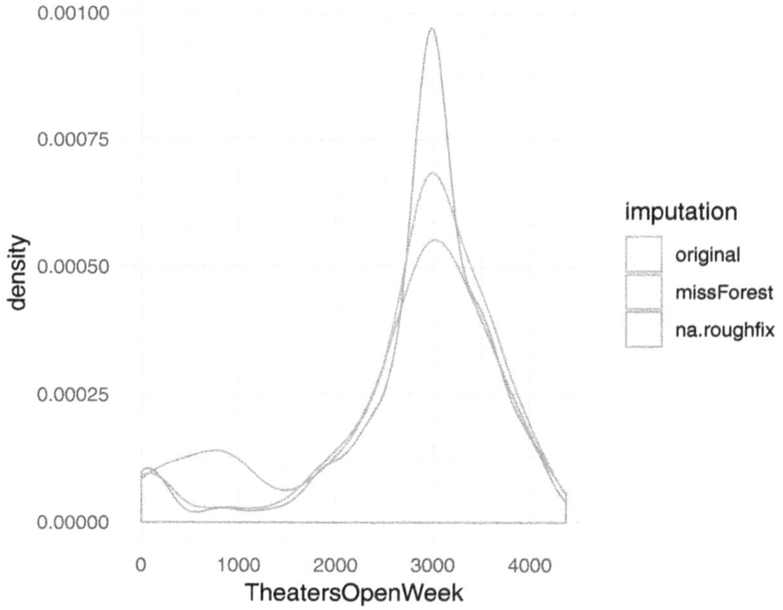

Figure 50: Comparing imputation methods (numeric variable)

- The orange curve shows the distribution after the imputation based on the `missForest` package.

- The blue shows the imputation method we discussed at the beginning, which replaces all `NA` by the median using the `na.roughfix` function in the `randomForest` package.
- The green one shows the distribution without any imputation (of course, NA values are not displayed).

Analysis:

Replacement of `NA` by the median tends to concentrate, as expected, all the values around 3000. On the other side, the imputation given by the missForest package provides a **more natural distribution** because it doesn't concentrate around a single value. That's why the peak around 3000 is lower than the original one.

The orange and green look pretty similar!

If we want to take an analytical point of view, then we can run a statistical test to compare, for example, the means or the variance.

Next we'll visualize `TheatersOpenWeek` discretized custom variable (`TheatersOpenWeek_cat_cust`).

```
# An ugly hack to plot NA as a category
levels(df_all$TheatersOpenWeek_cat_cust)=
  c(levels(df_all$TheatersOpenWeek_cat_cust), "NA")

flag_na=is.na(df_all$TheatersOpenWeek_cat_cust)

df_all$TheatersOpenWeek_cat_cust[flag_na]="NA"

# Now the plot!
ggplot(df_all, aes(x = TheatersOpenWeek_cat_cust,
                   fill = TheatersOpenWeek_cat_cust)
      ) +
  geom_bar(na.rm=T) +
```

```
facet_wrap(~imputation) +
geom_text(stat='count',
          aes(label=..count..),
          vjust=-1) +
ylim(0, 125) +
scale_fill_brewer(palette="Set2") +
theme_minimal() +
theme(axis.text.x=
          element_text(angle = 45, hjust = 0.7)
      ) +
theme(legend.position="bottom")
```

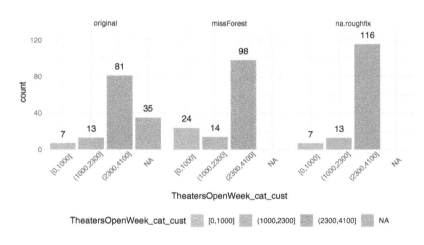

Figure 51: Comparing imputation methods

Analysis:

The original variable contains 35 NA values that were replaced using the mode or most frequent value in **na.roughfix**: (2300, 4100]. On the other hand we got an slighlty different result using **missForest**,

185

the completeness was based on other variables.

`missForest` added 15 rows in the category `[0, 1000]`, 3 in `[1000, 2300]`, and 17 in the `[2300, 4100]` category.

2.5.9.2 Method 2: Using the MICE approach

Advice: For the very first approach to missing value imputation, this method is really complex 😵.

MICE stands for "Multivariate Imputation by Chained Equations" also known as "Fully Conditional Specification". This book covers it due to its popularity.

MICE entails a complete framework to analyze and deal with missing values. It considers the interactions among **all variables** at the same time (multivariate and not just one) and bases its functionality on an **iterative** process that uses different predictive models to fill each variable.

Internally, it fills variable A, based on B and C. Then, it fills B based on A and C (A is previously predicted) and the iteration continues. The name "chained equations" comes from the fact that we can specify the algorithm per variable to impute the cases.

This creates M replications of the original data with no missing values. *But why create M replications?*

In each replication, the decision of what value to insert in the *empty slot* is based on the distribution.

Many MICE demonstrations focus on validating the imputation and using the predictive models that support the package, which number only a few. This is great if we don't want to use other predictive models (random forest, gradient boosting machine, etc.), or a cross-validation technique (e.g., `caret`).

The MICE technique puts the final result by setting a `pool()` function that averages the parameters (or betas) of the M predictive models providing facilities for measuring the variance due to missing values.

Yes, one model per each generated data frame. Sounds like bagging[37], isn't it? But we don't have this possibility with the mentioned models.

MICE has many functions to help us process and validate the filling results. But, to keep it very simple, we'll cover just a little part of it. The following example will focus on extracting a **data frame with no missing values ready to be used** with other programs or predictive models.

Example in R:

This will impute data for the **nhanes** data frame coming in mice package[38]. Let's check it:

```
# install.packages('mice')
library(mice)
df_status(nhanes)
```

```
##    variable q_zeros p_zeros q_na p_na q_inf p_inf
## 1       age       0       0    0    0     0     0
## 2       bmi       0       0    9   36     0     0
## 3       hyp       0       0    8   32     0     0
## 4       chl       0       0   10   40     0     0
##        type unique
## 1 numeric      3
## 2 numeric     16
## 3 numeric      2
## 4 numeric     13
```

Three variables have missing values. Let's fill them:

[37]https://en.wikipedia.org/wiki/Bootstrap_aggregating
[38]https://cran.r-project.org/web/packages/mice/mice.pdf

```
# Default imputation creates five complete datasets
imp_data = mice(nhanes, m = 5, printFlag = FALSE)

# Get a final dataset containing the five imputed data
# frames, total rows=nrow(nhanes)*5
data_all = complete(imp_data, "long")

# data_all contains the same columns as nhanes plus two
# more: .id and .imp .id=row number from 1 to 25
# .imp=imputation data frame .id 1 to 5 (m parameter)
```

In the original data, **nhanes** has 25 rows and data_all contains 125 rows, which is the result of creating 5 (**m=5**) complete data frames of 25 rows each.

Time to check the results:

densityplot(imp_data)

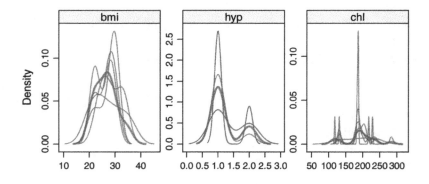

Figure 52: Analyzing missing values results using MICE

Each red line shows the distribution of each imputed data frame and the blue one contains the original distribution. The idea behind this is that if they look similar, then the imputation followed the original distribution.

For example, ch1 contains one imputed data frame; thus, only one red line containing two peaks around two values much higher than the original ones.

The drawbacks are it is a slow process that may require some tuning to work. For example: `mice_hollywood=mice(HollywoodMovies2011, m=5)` will fail after some time processing it and it is a small data frame.

More info regarding `MICE` package:

- Original MICE paper: Multivariate Imputation by Chained Equations in R[39]
- Handling missing data with MICE package; a simple approach[40]

2.5.10   Conclusions

After covering everything, we could ask: what is the best strategy? Well, it depends on how much we need to intervene in order to handle missing values.

A quick review of the strategies follows:

A) Excluding the rows and columns with missing values. Only applicable if there is *a few* rows (or columns) with missing values, **and** if the remaining data are enough to achieve the project goal. However, when we exclude rows with missing values and we build a predictive model that will run on production, when a **new case**

[39] https://www.jstatsoft.org/article/view/v045i03
[40] https://datascienceplus.com/handling-missing-data-with-mice-package-a-simple-approach

arrives that contains missing values, we must assign a value to process these.

B) The strategies of **converting numerical variables to categorical** and then creating the "empty" value (also applicable to categorical variables), is the quickest -and recommended- option to deal with empty valies. This way we introduce the missing values to the model so that it will handle the uncertainty.

C) The **imputation methods** like the ones we covered with MICE and missForest are considerably more complex. With these methods, we introduce a **controlled-bias** so that we don't have to exclude any rows or columns.

It's an art to find the correct balance between digging deeply into these transformations and keeping it simple. The invested time may not be reflected in the overall accuracy.

Regardless the method, it's quite important to analyze the impact of each decision. There is a lot of trial-and-error as well as exploratory data analysis leading up to the discovery of the most suitable method for your data and project.

Data Science Live Book

2.6 Considerations involving time

2.6.1 What is this about?

Everything changes and nothing stands still. - Heraclitus, (535 – 475 BC), pre-Socratic Greek philosopher.

So do variables.

As time goes by, variables may change their values, making the time-analysis crucial in order to create a predictive model. Avoiding the use of **effects** as **causes**.

What are we going to review in this chapter?

- Concepts of filtering information before the event to predict.
- How to analyze and prepare variables that increase -or decrease-their value to infinity (and beyond).

2.6.1.1 Don't use information from the future

Picture from the movie: "Back to the future" (1985). Robert Zemeckis (Director).

Using a variable which contains information **after** the event it's being predicted, is a common mistake when starting a new predictive model project, like playing the lottery today using the tomorrow's newspaper.

Imagine we need to build a predictive model to know what users are likely to adquire full subscription in a web application, and this software has a ficticious feature called it `feature_A`:

```
##    user_id feature_A full_subscription
## 1        1       yes               yes
## 2        2       yes               yes
## 3        3       yes               yes
## 4        4        no                no
## 5        5       yes               yes
## 6        6        no                no
## 7        7        no                no
## 8        8        no                no
## 9        9        no                no
## 10      10        no                no
```

We build the predictive model, we got a perfect accuracy, and an inspection throws the following: *"100% of users that have a full sub-*

scription, uses Feature A". Some predictive algorithms report variable importance; thus `feature_A` will be at the top.

The problem is: `feature_A` is only available **after the user goes for full subscription**. Therefore it cannot be used.

The key message is: Don't trust in perfect variables, nor perfect models.

2.6.1.2 Play fair with data, let it develop their behavior

Like in nature, things have a minimum and maximum time to start showing certain behavior. This time oscillates from 0 to infinity. In practice it's recommended to study what is the best period to analyze, in other words, we may exclude all the behavior before and after this observation period. To establish ranges in variables, it's not straight forward since it may be kind of subjective.

Imagine we've got a **numerical variable** which increases as time moves. We may need to define a **observation time window** to filter the data and feed the predictive model.

- Setting the **minimum** time: How much time is it need to start seeing the behavior?
- Setting the **maximum** time: How much time is it required to see the end of the behavior?

The easiest solution is: setting minimum since begin and the maximum as the whole history.

Case study:

Two people, `Ouro` and `Borus`, are users of a web application which has a certain functionality called `feature_A`, and we need to build a predictive model which forecast based on `feature_A` usage -measured in clicks- if the person is going to acquire `full_subscription`.

193

The current data says: Borus has `full_subscription`, while Ouro doesn't.

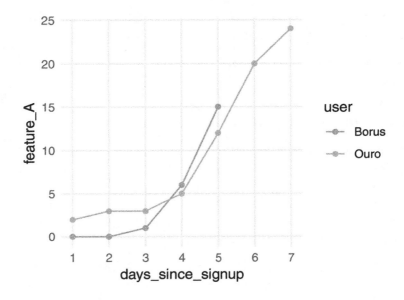

Figure 53: Be careful about time considerations

User `Borus` starts using `feature_A` from day 3, and after 5 days she has more use -15 vs. 12 clicks- on this feature than `Ouro` who started using it from day 0.

If `Borus` acquire `full subscription` and `Ouro` doesn't, *what would the model will learn?*

When modeling with full history -`days_since_signup` = `all`-, the higher the `days_since_signup` the higher the likelihood, since `Borus` has the highest number.

However, if we keep only with the user history corresponding to their first 5 days since signup, the conclusion is the opposite.

Why to keep first 5 days of history?

The behavior in this kick-off period may be more relevant -regarding prediction accuracy- than analyzing the whole history. It depends on each case as we said before.

2.6.1.3 Fighting the infinite

The number of examples on this topic is vast. Let's keep the essence of this chapter in **how data changes across time**. Sometimes it's straightforward, as a variable reaching its minimum (or maximum) after a fixed time length. This case is easily achievable.

On the other hand, it requires the human being to fight the infinite.

Consider the following example. *How much hours are needed to reach the 0 value?*

How about 100 hours?

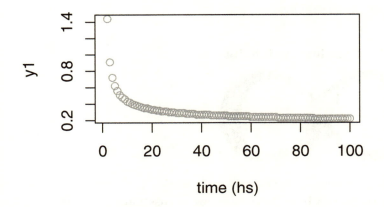

Figure 54: 100 hours

Hmm let's check the minimum value.

[1] "Min value after 100 hours: 0.22"

It's close to zero, but *what if we wait 1000 hours?*

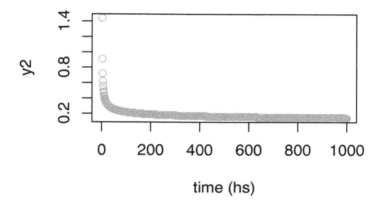

Figure 55: 1,000 hours

```
## [1] "Min value after 1,000 hours: 0.14"
```

Hurra! We are approaching it! From 0.21 to 0.14 But what if we wait 10 times more? (10,000 hours)

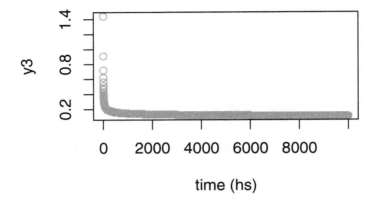

Figure 56: 10,000 hours

```
## [1] "Min value after 10,000 hours: 0.11"
```

Still no zero! How much time do I need?! 😱

As you may notice, it will probably reach the zero value in the infinity...
We are in the presence of an Asymptote[41].

What do we have to do? Time to go to the next section.

2.6.1.4 Befriend the infinite

The last example can be seen in the analysis of customer age in the
company. *This value can be infinite.*

For example, if the project goal is to predict a binary outcome, like

---

[41]https://en.wikipedia.org/wiki/Asymptote

198

buy/don't buy, one useful analysis is to calculate the buy rate according to age's user. Coming to conclusions like: *In average, a customer needs around 6 months to buy this product.*

This answer may come by the joint work of the data scientist and the domain expert.

In this case, a zero can be considered the same as the value which has the 95% of the population. In statistics terms it is the 0.95 **percentile**. This book extensively covers this topic in Annex 1: The magic of percentiles. This is a key topic in exploratory data analysis.

A related case is **dealing with outliers**, when we can apply this cutting percentile criteria, as we saw in the treating outliers chapter.

2.6.1.5 Examples in other areas

It's really common to find this kind of variables in many data sets or projects.

In medicine, the survival analysis projects[42], the doctors usually define a threshold of, for example, 3 years to consider that one patient *survive* the treatment.

In marketing projects, if a user decreases its activity under a certain threshold, let's say: * 10-clicks in company's web page during last month * Not opening an email after 1-week * If she (or he) don't buy after 30-days

Can be defined as a churned or lost opportunity customer.

In customer support, an issue can be marked as solved after the person doesn't complain during 1-week.

In brain signal analysis, if these signals come from the visual cortex in a project that, for example, we need to predict what type of image

---

[42]https://en.wikipedia.org/wiki/Survival_analysis

the patient is looking at, then the first 40ms of values are useless because it is time the brain need to start processing the signal.

But this also happens in *"real life"*, like the case when we write a data science book suitable for all ages, how much time is it required to end it? An infinite amount? Probably not 😄.

2.6.1.6 Final thoughts

Defining a time frame to create a training and validation set **is not a free-lunch** when the data is dynamic, as well as deciding how to handle variables that change over time. That's why the **Exploratory Data Analysis** is important in order to get in touch with the data we're analyzing.

Topics are inter-connected. Now, it's the time to mention the relationship of this chapter with the assessing model performance Out-of-time Validation. When we predict events in the future, we have to analyze how much time is it needed for the target variable to change.

The key concept here: **how to handle time in predictive modeling**. It's a good opportunity to ask: *How would it be possible to address this time issues with automatic systems?*

Human knowledge is crucial in these contexts to define thresholds based on experience, intuition and some calculations.

Data Science Live Book

3 Selecting Best Variables

3.1 General Aspects in Selecting Best Variables

3.1.1 What is this about?

This chapter covers the following topics:

- The best variables ranking from conventional machine learning algorithms, either predictive or clustering.
- The nature of selecting variables with and without predictive models.
- The effect of variables working in groups (intuition and information theory).
- Exploring the best variable subset in practice using R.

Selecting the best variables is also known as feature selection, selecting the most important predictors, selecting the best predictors, among others.

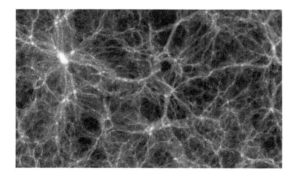

Figure 57: As above, so below

Image: Is it a neural network? Nope. Dark matter, from the "The Millennium Simulation Project".

3.2 Intuition

Selecting the best variables is like doing a summary of a story, we want to focus on those few details that best describe what we're talking about. The balance threads between talking *too much* about unnecessary details (overfitting) and talking *too little* about the essence of the story (underfitting).

Another example can be the decision of buying a new laptop: *what are the features that we care about the most? Price, color and shipping method? Color and battery life? Or just price?*

From the **Information Theory** point of view -a key point in machine learning-, the data that we are working on has **entropy** (chaos). When we select variables, we are are reducing the entropy of our system by adding information.

3.3 The "best" selection?

The chapter says "best", but we'd better mention a conceptual point, in general terms *there is no unique best variable selection.*

To start from this perspective is important, since in the exploration of many algorithms that *rank* the variables according to their predictive power, we can find different -and similar- results. That is:

- Algorithm 1 has chosen as the best variable var_1, followed by var_5 and var_14.
- Algorithm 2 did this ranking: var_1, var_5 and var_3.

Let's imagine, based on algorithm 1, the accuracy is 80%, while the accuracy based on algorithm 2 is 78%. Considering that every model has its inner variance, the result can be seen as the same.

This perspective can help us to reduce time in pursuing the perfect variable selection.

However going to the extremes, there will be a set of variables that will rank high across many algorithms, and the same goes for those with little predictive power. After several runs most reliable variables will emerge quickly, so:

Conclusion: If results are not good the focus should be on improving and checking the **data preparation** step. *The next section will exemplify it.*

3.3.1 Going deeper into variable ranking

It's quite common to find in literature and algorithms, that covers this topic an univariate analysis, which is a ranking of variables given a particular metric.

We're going to create two models: random forest and gradient boosting machine (GBM) using `caret` R package to cross-validate the data. Next, we'll compare the best variable ranking that every model returns.

```
library(caret)
library(funModeling)
library(dplyr)

# Excluding all NA rows from the data, in this case, NAs
# are not the main issue to solve, so we'll skip the 6
# cases which have NA (or missing values).
heart_disease = na.omit(heart_disease)

# Setting a 4-fold cross-validation
fitControl = trainControl(method = "cv", number = 4,
  classProbs = TRUE, summaryFunction = twoClassSummary)
```

```r
# Creating the random forest model, finding the best
# tuning parameter set
set.seed(999)
fit_rf = train(x = select(heart_disease,
  -has_heart_disease, -heart_disease_severity),
  y = heart_disease$has_heart_disease,
  method = "rf", trControl = fitControl,
  verbose = FALSE, metric = "ROC")

# Creating the gradient boosting machine model, finding
# the best tuning parameter set
fit_gbm = train(x = select(heart_disease,
  -has_heart_disease, -heart_disease_severity),
  y = heart_disease$has_heart_disease, method = "gbm",
  trControl = fitControl, verbose = FALSE,
  metric = "ROC")
```

Now we can proceed with the comparison.

The columns `importance_rf` and `importance_gbm` represent the importance measured by each algorithm. Based on each metric, there are `rank_rf` and `rank_gbm` which represent the importance order, finally `rank_diff` (`rank_rf` - `rank_gbm`) represents how different each algorithm rank the variables.

```r
# Here we manipulate to show a nice the table described
# before
var_imp_rf = data.frame(varImp(fit_rf,
  scale = T)["importance"]) %>%
  dplyr::mutate(variable = rownames(.)) %>%
  dplyr::rename(importance_rf = Overall) %>%
  dplyr::arrange(-importance_rf) %>%
  dplyr::mutate(rank_rf = seq(1:nrow(.)))
```

```
var_imp_gbm = as.data.frame(varImp(fit_gbm,
  scale = T)["importance"]) %>%
  dplyr::mutate(variable = rownames(.)) %>%
  dplyr::rename(importance_gbm = Overall) %>%
  dplyr::arrange(-importance_gbm) %>%
  dplyr::mutate(rank_gbm = seq(1:nrow(.)))
final_res = merge(var_imp_rf, var_imp_gbm,
  by = "variable")

final_res$rank_diff = final_res$rank_rf -
  final_res$rank_gbm

# Printing the results!
final_res
```

variable	importance_rf	rank_rf	importance_gbm	rank_gbm	rank_diff
exter_angina	29.15468	11	11.544326	6	5
slope	37.44874	10	20.799135	5	5
gender	21.72545	12	5.557935	9	3
chest_pain	97.85192	3	100.000000	1	2
fasting_blood_sugar	0.00000	14	0.000000	13	1
oldpeak	89.31555	5	51.556053	4	1
resting_blood_pressure	57.47780	8	5.690607	8	0
thal	98.15852	2	91.395284	2	0
exer_angina	37.68362	9	5.106130	10	-1
resting_electro	9.09967	13	0.000000	14	-1
num_vessels_flour	100.00000	1	88.478330	3	-2
max_heart_rate	96.89898	4	6.697837	7	-3
serum_cholestoral	62.03931	7	3.344057	11	-4
age	76.10440	6	3.140659	12	-6

Figure 58: Comparing different variable ranking

We can see that there are variables which are not important at all to both models (`fasting_blood_sugar`). There are others that maintain a position at the top of importance like `chest_pain` and `thal`.

Different predictive model implementations have their criteria to report what are the best features, according to that particular model. This ends up in different ranking across different algorithms. *More info about the inner importance metrics can be found at the caret documentation*[43].

Even more, in tree based models like GBM and Random Forest there is a random component to picking up variables, and the importance is based on prior -and automatic- variable selection when building the trees. The importance of each variable depends on the others, not only on its isolated contribution: **Variables work in groups**. We'll back on this later on this chapter.

Although the ranking will vary from algorithm to algorithm, in general terms there is a correlation between all of these results as we mentioned before.

Conclusion: Every ranking list is not the *"final truth"*, it gives us orientation about where the information is.

3.4 The nature of the selection

There are two main approaches when doing variable selection:

Predictive model dependent:

Like the ones we saw before, this is the most common. The model will rank variables according to one intrinsic measure of accuracy. In tree-based models, metrics such as information gain, Gini index, node impurity. More info at (stackoverflow.com 2017) and (stats.stackexchange.com 2017a).

---

[43] https://topepo.github.io/caret/variable-importance.html

Not predictive model dependent:

This is interesting since they are not as popular as the other ones, but they are proved to perform really well in areas related to genomic data. They need to find those *relevant* genes (input variable) that are correlated with some disease, like cancer (target variable).

Data from this area is characterized by having a huge number of variables (in the order of thousands), which is much bigger than problems in other areas.

One algorithm to perform this is mRMR[44], acronym for Minimum Redundancy Maximum Relevance Feature Selection. It has its own implementation in R in mRMRe[45] package.

Another not model-depandent algorithm is `var_rank_info`, a function provided by funModeling[46] package. It ranks the variables according to several **information theory** metrics. An example will be presented later on.

3.5 Improving variables

Variables can increase their predictive power by treating them.

This book covers by now:

- Improvement of categorical variables.
- Reducing the noise in numerical variables through binning in the chapter: Discretizing numerical variables.
- How to deal with outliers in R.
- Missing Data: Analysis, Handling, and Imputation of

---

[44]http://home.penglab.com/proj/mRMR
[45]https://cran.r-project.org/web/packages/mRMRe/vignettes/mRMRe.pdf
[46]https://cran.r-project.org/web/packages/funModeling/funModeling.pdf

3.6   Cleaning by domain knowledge

It's not related to algorithmic procedures, but to the area from which the data comes.

Imagine data coming from a survey. This survey has one year of history, and during the first three months there was no good process control. When inserting data users could type whatever they wanted. Variables during this period will probably be spurious.

It's easy to recognize it when during a given period of time, the variable comes empty, null or with extreme values.

We should then ask a question:

Is this data reliable? Keep in mind the predictive model will learn *as a kid*, it will not judge the data, just learn from it. If data is spurious in a given period of time, then we may remove these input cases.

To go further on this point, we should do a deeper exploratory data analysis. Both numerically and graphically.

3.7 Variables work in groups

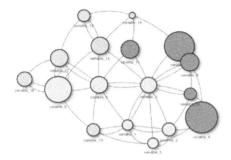

Figure 59: Variables work in groups

When selecting the *best* variables, the main aim is to get those variables which carry the most information regarding a target, outcome or dependent variable.

A predictive model will find its weights or parameters based on its 1 to 'N' input variables.

Variables usually don't work isolated when explaining an event. Quoting Aristotle:

> "The whole is greater than the sum of its parts."

This is also true when selecting the *best* features:

Building a predictive model with two variables may reach a higher accuracy than the models built with only one variable.

For example: Building a model based on variable `var_1` could lead to an overall accuracy of 60%. On the other hand, building a model based on `var_2` could reach an accuracy of 72%. But when we combine these

209

two `var_1` and `var_2` variables, we could achieve an accuracy above 80%.

3.7.1   Example in R: Variables working in groups

Aristotle (384 - 322 BC).
Philosopher and Data Scientist.

Figure 60: Aristotle (384 BC–322 BC)

The following code illustrates what Aristotle said *some* years ago.

It creates 3 models based on different variable subsets:

- model 1 is based on `max_heart_rate` input variable
- model 2 is based on `chest_pain` input variable
- model 3 is based on `max_heart_rate` **and** `chest_pain` input variables

Each model returns the metric ROC, and the result contains the improvement of considering the two variables at the same time vs. taking each variable isolated.

```
library(caret)
library(funModeling)
library(dplyr)
```

```r
# setting cross-validation 4-fold
fitControl =
  trainControl(method = "cv",
               number = 4,
               classProbs = TRUE,
               summaryFunction = twoClassSummary
               )

create_model<-function(input_variables)
{
  # create gradient boosting machine model
  # based on input variables
  fit_model = train(x=select(heart_disease,
                             one_of(input_variables)
                             ),
             y = heart_disease$has_heart_disease,
             method = "gbm",
             trControl = fitControl,
             verbose = FALSE,
             metric = "ROC")

  # returning the ROC as the performance metric
  max_roc_value=max(fit_model$results$ROC)
  return(max_roc_value)
}

roc_1=create_model("max_heart_rate")
roc_2=create_model("chest_pain")
roc_3=create_model(c("max_heart_rate", "chest_pain"))

avg_improvement=round(100*(((roc_3-roc_1)/roc_1)+
                          ((roc_3-roc_2)/roc_2))/2,
```

```
avg_improvement_text=sprintf("Average improvement: %s%%",
                             avg_improvement)

results =
  sprintf("ROC model based on 'max_heart_rate': %s.;
  based on 'chest_pain': %s; and based on both: %s",
  round(roc_1,2),
  round(roc_2,2),
  round(roc_3, 2)
  )

# printing the results!
cat(c(results, avg_improvement_text), sep="\n\n")

## ROC model based on 'max_heart_rate': 0.74.;
##    based on 'chest_pain': 0.76; and based on both: 0.81
##
## Average improvement: 7.79%
```

3.7.2   Tiny example (based on Information Theory)

Consider the following *big data* table 😄4 rows, 2 input variables (var_1, var_2) and one outcome (target):

var_1	var_2	target
a	x	red
a	z	blue
b	x	blue
b	z	red

Figure 61: Unity gives strength: Combining variables

If we build a predictive model based on **var_1** only, what it will *see?*, the value a is correlated with output **blue** and **red** in the same proportion (50%):

- If var_1='a' then likelihood of target='red' is 50% (row 1)
- If var_1='b' then likelihood of target='blue' is 50% (row 2)

Same analysis goes for var_2

When the same input is related to different outcomes it's defined as **noise**. The intuition is the same as one person telling us: *"Hey it's going to rain tomorrow!"*, and another one saying: *"For sure tomorrow it's not going to rain"*. We'd think... *"OMG! do I need the umbrella or not 😱?"*

Going back to the example, taking the two variables at the same time, the correspondence between the input and the output in unique: "If var_1='a' and var_2='x' then the likelihood of being **target='red'** is 100%". You can try other combinations.

Summing-up:

That was an example of **variables working in groups**, considering var_1 and var_2 at the same time increases the predictive power.

Nonetheless, it's a deeper topic to cover, considering the last analysis; how about taking an **Id** column (every value is unique) to predict something? The correspondence between input-output will also be unique... but is it a useful model? There'll be more to come about information theory in this book.

3.7.3 Conclusions

- The proposed R example based on `heart_disease` data shows an average **improvement of 9%** when considering two variables at a time, not too bad. This percentage of improvement is the result of the **variables working in groups**.
- This effect appears if the variables contain information, such is the case of `max_heart_rate` and `chest_pain` (or `var_1` and `var_2`).
- Putting **noisy variables** next to good variables **will usually affect** overall performance.
- Also the **work in groups** effect is higher if the input variables **are not correlated between** them. This is difficult to optimize in practice. More on this on the next section...

3.7.4 Rank best features using information theory

As introduced at the beginning of the chapter, we can get variable importance without using a predictive model using information theory.

From version 1.6.6 the package `funModeling` introduces the function `var_rank_info`, which takes two arguments, the data and the target variable, because it follows:

```
variable_importance =
  var_rank_info(heart_disease, "has_heart_disease")

# Printing results
variable_importance
```

```
##                           var    en    mi           ig
## 1   heart_disease_severity 1.846 0.995 0.9950837595
## 2                     thal 2.032 0.209 0.2094550580
## 3               exer_angina 1.767 0.139 0.1391389302
## 4              exter_angina 1.767 0.139 0.1391389302
## 5               chest_pain 2.527 0.205 0.2050188327
## 6          num_vessels_flour 2.381 0.182 0.1815217813
## 7                    slope 2.177 0.112 0.1124219069
## 8         serum_cholestoral 7.481 0.561 0.5605556771
## 9                   gender 1.842 0.057 0.0572537665
## 10                  oldpeak 4.874 0.249 0.2491668741
## 11           max_heart_rate 6.832 0.334 0.3336174096
## 12 resting_blood_pressure 5.567 0.143 0.1425548155
## 13                      age 5.928 0.137 0.1371752885
## 14          resting_electro 2.059 0.024 0.0241482908
## 15     fasting_blood_sugar 1.601 0.000 0.0004593775
##              gr
## 1  0.5390655068
## 2  0.1680456709
## 3  0.1526393841
## 4  0.1526393841
## 5  0.1180286190
## 6  0.1157736478
## 7  0.0868799615
## 8  0.0795557228
## 9  0.0632970555
## 10 0.0603576874
## 11 0.0540697329
## 12 0.0302394591
## 13 0.0270548944
## 14 0.0221938072
## 15 0.0007579095
```

```
# Plotting
ggplot(variable_importance,
       aes(x = reorder(var, gr),
           y = gr, fill = var)
       ) +
  geom_bar(stat = "identity") +
  coord_flip() +
  theme_bw() +
  xlab("") +
  ylab("Variable Importance
       (based on Information Gain)"
       ) +
  guides(fill = FALSE)
```

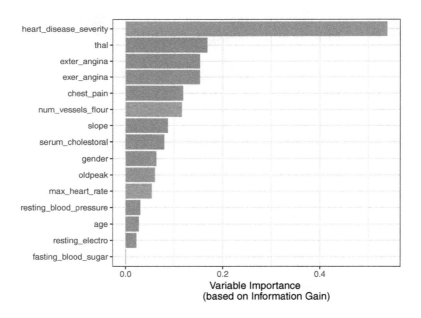

Figure 62: Variable Importance (based on Gain Ratio)

Is `heart_disease_severity` the feature that explains the target the most?

No, this variable was used to generate the target, thus we must exclude it. It is a typical mistake when developing a predictive model to have either an input variable that was built in the same way as the target (as in this case) or adding variables from the future as explained in Considerations involving time.

Going back to the result of `var_rank_info`, the resulting metrics come from information theory:

- `en`: entropy measured in bits
- `mi`: mutual information
- `ig`: information gain
- `gr`: gain ratio

We are not going to cover what is behind these metrics at this point as this will be covered exclusively in a future chapter, However, the **gain ratio** is the most important metric here, ranged from 0 to 1, with higher being better.

Fuzzy boundaries

We've just seen how to calculate importance based on information theory metrics. This topic is not exclusive to this chapter; this concept is also present in the Exploratory Data Analysis - Correlation and Relationship section.

To *select best features* is related to *exploratory data analysis* and vice-versa.

3.8 Correlation between input variables

The ideal scenario is to build a predictive model with only variables not correlated between them. In practice, it's complicated to keep such

217

a scenario for all variables.

Usually there will be a set of variables that are not correlated between them, but also there will be others that have at least some correlation.

In practice a suitable solution would be to exclude those variables with a **remarkably high-level** of correlation.

Regarding how to measure correlation. Results can be highly different based on linear or non-linear procedures. More info at the Correlation

What is the problem with adding correlated variables?

The problem is that we're adding complexity to the model: it's usually more time-consuming, harder to understand, less explainable, less accurate, etc. This is an effect we reviewed in Don't predictive models handle high cardinality?. The general rule would be: Try to add the top N variables that are correlated with the output but not correlated between them. This leads us to the next section.

3.9 Keep it simple

Figure 63: Fractals in Nature

Nature operates in the shortest way possible. -Aristotle.

The principle of **Occam's razor**: Among competing hypotheses, the one with the fewest assumptions should be selected.

Re-interpreting this sentence for machine learning, those "hypotheses" can be seen as variables, so we've got:

Among different predictive models, the one with fewest variables should be selected. (Wikipedia 2017c)

Of course, there is also the trade-off of adding-substracting variables and the accuracy of the model.

A predictive model with a *high* number of variables will tend to do **overfitting**. While on the other hand, a model with a *low* number of variables will lead to doing **underfitting**.

The concept of *high* and *low* is **highly subjective** to the data that is being analyzed. In practice, we may have some accuracy metric, for example, the ROC value. i.e. we would see something like:

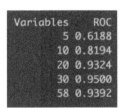

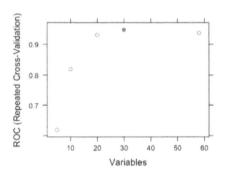

Figure 64: ROC values for different variables subset

The last picture shows the ROC accuracy metric given different subsets of variables (5, 10, 20, 30 and 58). Each dot represents the ROC value given a certain number of variables used to build the model.

We can check that the highest ROC appears when the model is built with 30 variables. If we based the selection only on an automated process, we might be choosing a subset which tends to overfit the data. This report was produced by library **caret** in R ((Kuhn 2017) but is analogous to any software.

Take a closer look at the difference between the subset of 20 and the 30; there is only an improvement of **1.8%** -from 0.9324 to 0.95- choosing **10 more variables.** In other words: *Choosing 50% more variables will impact in less than 2% of improvement.*

Even more, this 2% may be an error margin given the variance in the prediction that every predictive model has, as we seen in Knowing the error chapter.

Conclusion:

In this case, and being consequent with Occam's Razor principle, the best solution is to build the model with the subset of 20 variables.

Explaining to others -and understanding- a model with 20 variables is easier than the similar one with 30.

3.10 Variable selection in Clustering?

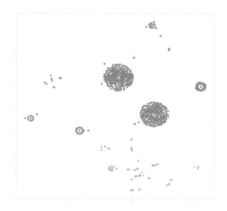

Figure 65: Example of cluster segmentation

This concept usually appears only in predictive modeling, i.e. having some variables to predict a target one. In clustering there is no target variable, we let the data speak, and the natural segments arise according to some distance metric.

However, **not every variable contributes in the same way to the dissimilarity in the cluster model**. Keeping it brief, if we have 3 clusters as output, and we measure the average of each variable, we expect to have these averages *quite* dissimilar between them, right?

Having built 2 cluster models, in the first one the averages of the **age** variable is 24, 33 and 26 years; while on the second one we have: 23, 31 and 46. In the second model the variable **age** is having more variability, thus it is more relevant to the model.

This was just an example considering two models, but it's the same considering just one. Those variables with **more distance** across averages will tend to **define better** the cluster than the others.

Unlike predictive modeling, in clustering *less important* variables shouldn't be removed, those variables aren't important in that particular model, but they could be if we build another one with other parameters. The cluster models' quality is highly subjective.

Finally, we could run, for example, a random forest model with the cluster as a target variable and in this way quickly collect the most important variables.

3.11   Selecting the best variables in practice

3.11.1   The short answer

Pick up the top N variables from the algorithm you're using and then re-build the model with this subset. Not every predictive model retrieves variable rankings, but if it does, use the same model (for example gradient boosting machine) to get the ranking and to build the final model.

For those models like k-nearest neighbors which don't have a built-in select best features procedure, it's valid to use the selection of another algorithm. It will lead to better results than using all the variables.

3.11.2   The long answer

- When possible, **validate** the list with someone who knows about the context, the business or the data source. Either for the top N or the bottom M variables. As regards those *bad* variables, we may be missing something in the data munging that could be destroying their predictive power.

- Understand each variable, its meaning in context (business, medical, other).
- Do **exploratory data analysis** to see the distributions of the most important variables regarding a target variable, *does the selection make sense?* If the target is binary then the function Profiling target using cross_plot can be used.
- Does the average of any variable *significantly* change over time? Check for abrupt changes in distributions.
- Suspect about high cardinality top-ranked variables (like postal code, let's say above +100 categories). More information at High Cardinality Variable in Predictive Modeling.
- When making the selection -as well as a predictive modeling-, try and use methods which contain some mechanism of re-sampling (like bootstrapping), and cross-validation. More information in the knowing the error chapter.
- Try other methods to find **groups of variables**, like the one mentioned before: mRMR.
- If the selection doesn't meet the needs, try creating new variables, you can check the **data preparation** chapter. Coming soon: Feature engineering chapter.

3.11.3 Generate your own knowledge

It's difficult to generalize when the nature of the data is so different, from **genetics** in which there are thousands of variables and a few rows, to web-navigation when new data is coming all the time.

The same applies to the objective of the analysis. Is it to be used in a competition where precision is highly necessary? Perhaps the solution may include more correlated variables in comparison to an ad-hoc study in which the primary goal is a simple explanation.

There is no one-size-fits-all answer to face all possible challenges; you'll find powerful insights using your experience. It's just a matter of practice.

Data Science Live Book

3.12 Target profiling

3.12.1 Using `cross_plot` (dataViz)

3.12.1.1 What is this about?

This plot intent to show in real scenarios if a variable is or not important, making a visual summary of it, *(by grouping numerical variables into bins/groups).*

3.12.1.2 Example 1: Is gender correlated with heart disease?

```
cross_plot(heart_disease, input = "gender",
  target = "has_heart_disease")
```

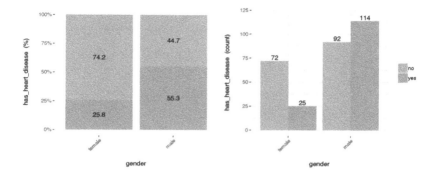

Figure 66: Using cross-plot to analyze and report variable importance

Last two plots have the same data source, showing the distribution of `has_heart_disease` regarding `gender`. The one on the left shows in percentage value, while the one on the right shows in absolute value.

3.12.1.2.1 How to extract conclusions from the plots? (Short version)

`Gender` variable seems to be a **good predictor**, since the likelihood of having heart disease is different given the female/male groups. **it gives an order to the data**.

3.12.1.3 How to extract conclusions from the plots? (Long version)

From 1st plot (%):

1. The **likelihood** of having heart disease for males is 55.3%, while for females is: 25.8%.
2. The heart disease rate for males **doubles** the rate for females (55.3 vs. 25.8, respectively).

225

From 2nd plot (count):

1. There is a total of **97 females**:
   - 25 of them have heart disease (25/97=25.8%, which is the ratio of the 1st plot).
   - the remaining 72 have not heart disease (74.2%)
2. There is a total of **206 males**:
   - 114 of them have heart disease (55.3%)
   - the remaining 92 have not heart disease (44.7%)
3. Total cases: Summing the values of four bars: 25+72+114+92=**303**.

*Note: What would it happened if instead of having the rates of 25.8% vs. 55.3% (female vs. male), they had been more similar like 30.2% vs. 30.6%). In this case variable **gender** it would have been much less relevant, since it doesn't separate the **has_heart_disease** event.*

3.12.1.4   Example 2: Crossing with numerical variables

Numerical variables should be **binned** to plot them with a histogram, otherwise, the plot is not showing information, as it can be seen here:

3.12.1.4.1   Equal frequency binning

There is a function included in the package (inherited from Hmisc package): `equal_freq`, which returns the bins/buckets based on the **equal frequency criteria**. Which is -*or tries to*- have the same quantity of rows per bin.

For numerical variables, `cross_plot` has by default the `auto_binning=T`, which automatically calls the `equal_freq` function with `n_bins=10` (or the closest number).

```
cross_plot(heart_disease, input = "max_heart_rate",
  target = "has_heart_disease")
```

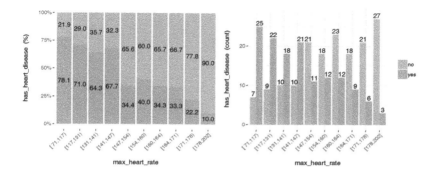

Figure 67: Numeric variable as input (automatic binning)

3.12.1.5   Example 3: Manual binning

If you don't want the automatic binning, then set the `auto_binning=F` in `cross_plot` function.

For example, creating `oldpeak_2` based on equal frequency, with three buckets.

```
heart_disease$oldpeak_2 =
  equal_freq(var=heart_disease$oldpeak, n_bins = 3)
summary(heart_disease$oldpeak_2)
```

```
## [0.0,0.2) [0.2,1.5) [1.5,6.2]
##      106       107        90
```

Plotting the binned variable (`auto_binning = F`):

```
cross_oldpeak_2 = cross_plot(heart_disease,
  input = "oldpeak_2", target = "has_heart_disease",
  auto_binning = F)
```

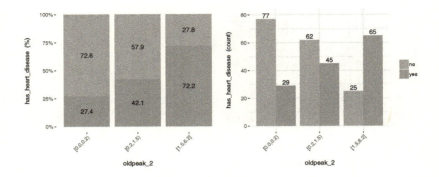

Figure 68: Disabling automatic binning shows the original variable

3.12.1.5.1 Conclusion

This new plot based on `oldpeak_2` shows clearly how: the likelihood of **having heart disease increases** as **oldpeak_2 increases** as well. *Again, it gives an order to the data.*

3.12.1.6 Example 4: Noise reducing

Converting variable `max_heart_rate` into a one of 10 bins:

```
heart_disease$max_heart_rate_2 =
  equal_freq(var=heart_disease$max_heart_rate, n_bins = 10)

cross_plot(heart_disease,
           input="max_heart_rate_2",
           target="has_heart_disease"
           )
```

228

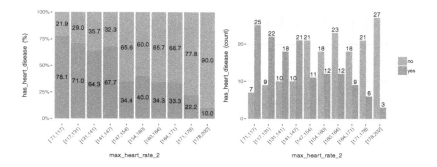

Figure 69: Plotting using custom binning

At first glance, `max_heart_rate_2` shows a negative and linear relationship. However, there are some buckets which add noise to the relationship. For example, the bucket (141, 146] has a higher heart disease rate than the previous bucket, and it was expected to have a lower. *This could be noise in data.*

Key note: One way to reduce the **noise** (at the cost of **losing** some information), is to split with less bins:

```
heart_disease$max_heart_rate_3 =
  equal_freq(var=heart_disease$max_heart_rate, n_bins = 5)

cross_plot(heart_disease,
            input="max_heart_rate_3",
            target="has_heart_disease"
            )
```

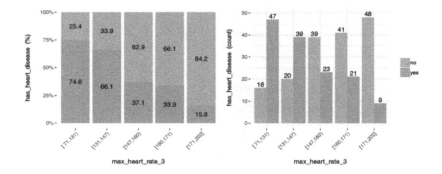

Figure 70: Reducing the bins may help to better expose the relationship

Conclusion: As it can be seen, now the relationship is much clean and clear. Bucket *'N'* has a higher rate than *'N+1'*, which implies a negative correlation.

How about saving the cross_plot result into a folder?

Just set the parameter **path_out** with the folder you want -It creates a new one if it doesn't exists-.

```
cross_plot(heart_disease, input = "max_heart_rate_3",
    target = "has_heart_disease", path_out = "my_plots")
```

It creates the folder **my_plots** into the working directory.

3.12.1.7 Example 5: cross_plot on multiple variables

Imagine you want to run cross_plot for several variables at the same time. To achieve this goal just define a vector containing the variable names.

If you want to analyze these 3 variables:

230

```
vars_to_analyze = c("age", "oldpeak", "max_heart_rate")

cross_plot(data = heart_disease,
  target = "has_heart_disease",
  input = vars_to_analyze)
```

3.12.1.8   Exporting plots

`plotar` and `cross_plot` can handle from 1 to N input variables, and plots generated by them can be easily exported in high quality with parameter **path_out**.

```
plotar(data = heart_disease, input = c("max_heart_rate",
  "resting_blood_pressure"), target = "has_heart_disease",
  plot_type = "boxplot", path_out = "my_awsome_folder")
```

Data Science Live Book

3.12.2   Using BoxPlots

3.12.2.1   What is this about?

The use of Boxplots in importance variable analysis gives a quick view of how different the quartiles are among the various values in a binary target variable.

```
# Loading funModeling !
library(funModeling)
data(heart_disease)

plotar(data = heart_disease, input = "age",
  target = "has_heart_disease", plot_type = "boxplot")
```

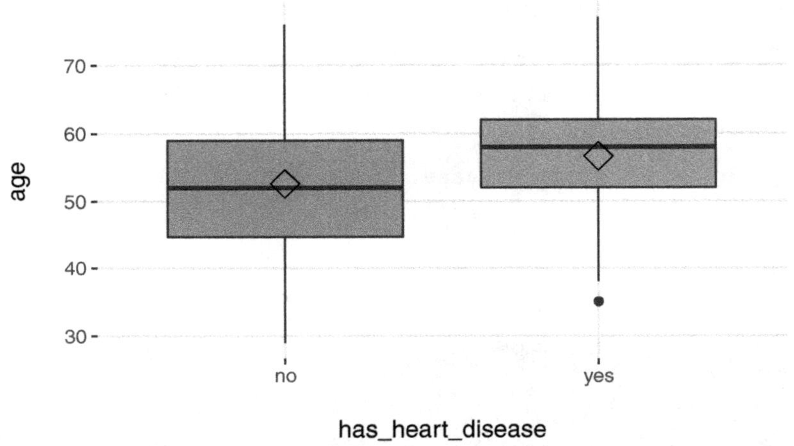

Figure 71: Profiling target using boxplot

*Rhomboid near the mean line represents the **median**.*

Box plot are used to see **percentiles graphically.**

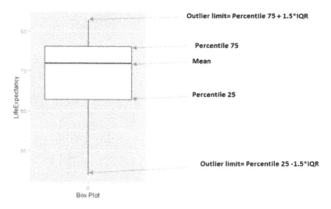

Figure 72: How to interpret a boxplot

When to use boxplots?

When we need to analyze different percentiles across the classes to predict. Note this is a powerful technique since the bias produced due to outliers doesn't affect as much as it does to the mean.

3.12.2.2 Boxplot: Good vs. Bad variable

Using more than one variable as inputs is useful in order to compare boxplots quickly, and thus getting the best variables. . .

```
plotar(data = heart_disease, input = c("max_heart_rate",
  "resting_blood_pressure"), target = "has_heart_disease",
  plot_type = "boxplot")
```

233

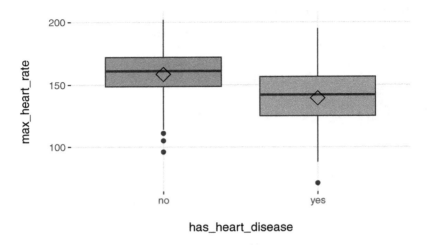

Figure 73: plotar function for multiple variables

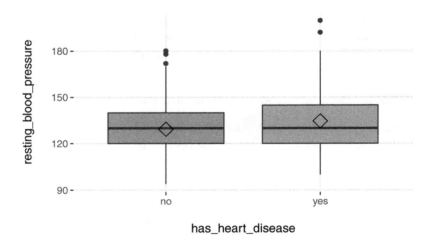

Figure 74: plotar function for multiple variables

We can conclude that `max_heart_rate` is a better predictor than `resting_blood_pressure`.

As a general rule, a variable will rank as **more important** if boxplots are **not aligned** horizontally.

Statistical tests: percentiles are another used feature used by them in order to determine -for example- if means across groups are or not the same.

3.12.2.3 Exporting plots

`plotar` and `cross_plot` can handle from 1 to N input variables, and plots generated by them can be easily exported in high quality with parameter **path_out**.

```
plotar(data = heart_disease, input = c("max_heart_rate",
  "resting_blood_pressure"), target = "has_heart_disease",
  plot_type = "boxplot", path_out = "my_awsome_folder")
```

- **Keep in mind this when using Histograms and BoxPlots**
  They are nice to see when the variable:
  - Has a good spread -not concentrated on a bunch of *3, 4..6..* different values, **and**
  - It has not extreme outliers... *(this point can be treated with* ***prep_outliers*** *function present in this package)*

3.12.3 Using Density Histograms

3.12.3.1 What is this about?

Density histograms are quite standard in any book/resource when plotting distributions. To use them in selecting variables gives a quick view on how well certain variable separates the class.

```
plotar(data = heart_disease, input = "age",
  target = "has_heart_disease", plot_type = "histdens")
```

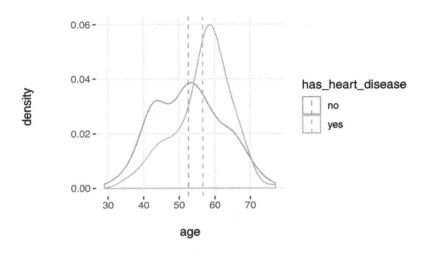

Figure 75: Profiling target using density histograms

Note: The dashed-line represents variable mean.

Density histograms are helpful to visualize the general shape of a numeric distribution.

This *general shape* is calculated based on a technique called **Kernel Smoother**, its general idea is to reduce high/low peaks (noise) present in near points/bars by estimating the function that describes the points. Here some pictures to illustrate the concept: https://en.wikipedia.org/wiki/Kernel_smoother

3.12.3.2 What is the relationship with a statistical test?

Something similar is what a **statistical test** sees: they measured **how**

236

different the curves are reflecting it in some statistics like the p-value using in the frequentist approach. It gives to the analyst reliable information to determine if the curves have -for example- the same mean.

3.12.3.3 Good vs. bad variable

```
plotar(data = heart_disease,
  input = c("resting_blood_pressure",
    "max_heart_rate"), target = "has_heart_disease",
  plot_type = "histdens")
```

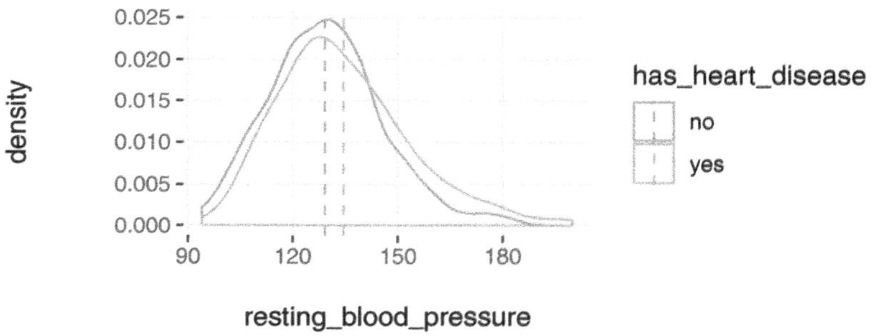

Figure 76: plotar function for multiple variables

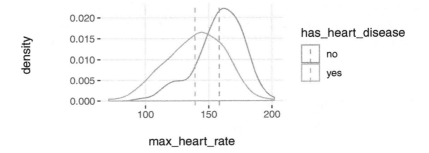

Figure 77: plotar function for multiple variables

And the model will see the same... if the curves are quite overlapped, like it is in `resting_blood_pressure`, then it's **not a good predictor** as if they were **more spaced** -like `max_heart_rate`.

- **Key in mind this when using Histograms & BoxPlots**
  They are nice to see when the variable:
  - Has a good spread -not concentrated on a bunch of *3, 4..6..* different values, **and**
  - It has not extreme outliers... *(this point can be treated with* `prep_outliers` *function present in this package)*

Data Science Live Book

238

4 Assesing Model Performance

It covers **methodological aspects of the error** in predictive models, how to measure it through **cross-validation** data and its similitude with **bootstrapping** technique. And how these strategies are used internally by some predictive models such us *random forest* or *gradient boosting machines*.

There is also a chapter about how to validate models when time is involved, which is similar to classical train/test validation.

4.1 Knowing the Error

Methodological Aspects on Model Validation

4.1.1 What's this about?

Once we've built a predictive model, how sure we are about its quality? Did it capture general patterns *-information-* (excluding the *-noise-*)?

4.1.1.1 What sort of data?

It has other approach rather than the one covered on Out-of-Time Validation. This approach could be used even when there is not possible to filter cases by date, for example having a data's snapshot at a certain point of time, when no new information will be generated.

For example some health data research from a reduced amount of people, a survey, or some data available on the internet for practicing purposes. It's either expensive, not practical, unethical or even impossible to add new cases. The `heart_disease` data coming in `funModeling` package is such an example.

4.1.2 Reducing unexpected behavior

When a model is trained, it just sees a part of reality. It's a sample from a population that cannot be entirely seen.

There are lots of ways to validate a model (Accuracy / ROC curves / Lift / Gain / etc). Any of these metrics are **attached to variance**, which implies **getting different values**. If we remove some cases and then fit a new model, we'll see a *slightly* different value.

Imagine we build a model and achieve an accuracy of `81`, now remove 10% of the cases, and then fit a new one, the accuracy now is: `78.4`. **What is the real accuracy?** The one obtained with 100% of data or the other based on 90%? For example, if the model will run live in a production environment, it will see **other cases** and the accuracy point will move to a new one.

So what is the real value? The one to report? **Re-sampling** and **cross-validation** techniques will average -based on different sampling and testing criteria- in order to retrieve an approximation to the most trusted value.

But why remove cases?

There is no sense in removing cases like that, but it gets an idea of how sensible the accuracy metric is, remember we're working with a sample from an unknown population.

If we'd have a fully deterministic model, a model that contains 100% of all cases we are studying, and predictions were 100% accurate in all cases, we wouldn't need all of this.

As far as we always analyze samples, we just need to getting closer to the *real and unknown truthness* of data through repetition, re-sampling, cross-validation, and so on...

4.1.3 Let's illustrate this with Cross-Validation (CV)

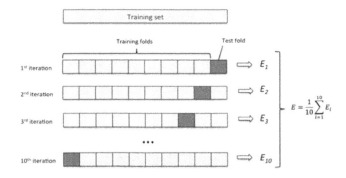

Figure 78: k-fold cross validation

Image credit: Sebastian Raschka Ref. (Raschka 2017)

4.1.3.1 CV short summary

- Splits the data into random groups, let's say 10, equally sized. These groups are commonly called `folds`, represented by the `'k'` letter.

241

- Take 9 folds, build a model, and then apply the model to the remaining fold (the one which was left out). This will return the accuracy metric we want: accuracy, ROC, Kappa, etc. We're using accuracy in this example.
- Repeat this k times (10 in our example). So we'll get 10 different accuracies. The final result will be the average of all of them.

This average will be the one to evaluate if a model is good or not, and also to include it in a report.

4.1.3.2   Practical example

There 150 rows in the `iris` data frame, using caret package[47] to build a **random forest** with `caret` using `cross-validation` will end up in the -internal- construction of 10 random forest, each one based on 135 rows (9/10 * 150), and reporting an accuracy based on remaining 15 (1/10 * 150) cases. This procedure is repeated 10 times.

This part of the output:

```
Resampling: Cross-Validated (10 fold)
Summary of sample sizes: 135, 135, 135, 135, 135, 135, ...
Resampling results:

  Accuracy   Kappa
  0.9466667  0.92
```

Figure 79: caret cross validation output

`Summary of sample sizes: 135, 135, 135, 135, 135, 135,`
..., each 135 represents a training sample, 10 in total but the output is truncated.

Rather a single number -the average-, we can see a distribution:

---

[47]http://topepo.github.io/caret/index.html

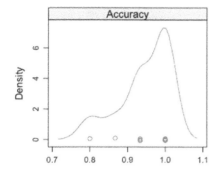

Figure 80: Visual analysis of the accuracy distribution

Min.	1st Qu.	Median	Mean	3rd Qu.	Max.
0.8667	0.9333	0.9333	0.9467	1.0000	1.0000

Figure 81: Accuracy distribution

- The min/max accuracy will be between ~0.8 and ~1.
- The mean is the one reported by `caret`.
- 50% of times it will be ranged between ~0.93 and ~1.

Recommended lecture by Rob Hyndman, creator of `forecast` package: *Why every statistician should know about cross-validation?* (Hyndman 2010)

4.1.4 But what is Error?

The sum of **Bias**, **Variance** and the ***unexplained error*** -inner noise-in data, or the one that the model will never be able to reduce.

These three elements represent the error reported.

4.1.4.1 What is the nature of Bias and Variance?

When the model doesn't work well, there may be several causes:

- **Model too complicated**: Let's say we have lots of input variables, which is related to **high variance**. The model will overfit on training data, having a poor accuracy on unseen data due to its particularization.
- **Model too simple**: On the other hand, the model may not be capturing all the information from the data due to its simplicity. This is related to **high bias**.
- **Not enough input data**: Data forms shapes in an n-dimensional space (where **n** is all the input+target variables). If there are not enough points, this shape is not developed well enough.

More info here in *"In Machine Learning, What is Better: More Data or better Algorithms"* (Amatriain 2015).

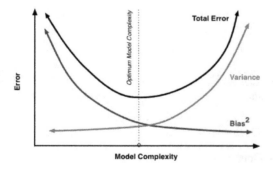

Figure 82: Bias vs. variance tradeoff

Image credit: Scott Fortmann-Roe (Fortmann 2012). It also contains an intuitive way of understanding error through bias and variance through a animation.

4.1.4.2 Complexity vs Accuracy Tradeoff

Bias and variance are related in the sense that if one goes down the other goes up, so it's a **tradeoff** between them. A practical example of this is on Akaike Information Criterion (AIC) model quality measure.

AIC is used as a heuristic to pick the best **time series model** in the `auto.arima` function inside `forecast` package in R (Hyndman 2017). It chooses the model with the lowest AIC.

The lower, the better: The accuracy in prediction will lower the value, while the number of parameters will increase it.

4.1.4.3 Bootstrapping vs Cross-Validation

- **Bootstrapping** is mostly used when estimating a parameter.
- **Cross-Validation** is the choice when choosing among different predictive models.

Note: For a deeper coverage about bias and variance, please go to (Fortmann 2012) and (Amatriain 2015) at the bottom of the page.

4.1.5 Any advice on practice?

It depends on the data, but it's common to find examples such as 10 fold CV, plus repetition: 10 fold CV, repeated 5 times. Other times we find: `5 fold CV, repeated 3 times`.

And using the average of the desired metric. It's also recommended to use the `ROC` for being less biased to unbalanced target variables.

Since these validation techniques are **time consuming**, consider choosing a model which will run fast, allowing model tunning, testing different configurations, trying different variables in a "short" amount of time. Random Forest[48] are an excellent option which gives **fast** and **accurate** results. More on Random Forest overall performance on (Fernandez-Delgado 2014).

Another good option is **gradient boosting machines**, it has more parameters to tune than random forest, but at least in R it's implementation works fast.

4.1.5.1 Going back to bias and variance

- Random Forest focuses on decreasing bias, while. . .
- Gradient boosting machine focuses on minimizing variance. More info in *"Gradient boosting machine vs random forest"* (stats.stackexchange.com 2015).

4.1.6 Don't forget: Data Preparation

Tweaking input data by transforming and cleaning it, will impact on model quality. Sometimes more than optimizing the model through its parameters.

Expand this point with the Data Preparation chapter.

---

[48] https://en.wikipedia.org/wiki/Random_forest

4.1.7 Final thoughts

- Validating the models through re-sampling / cross-validation helps us to estimate the "real" error present in the data. If the model runs in the future, that will be the expected error to have.
- Another advantage is **model tuning**, avoiding the overfitting in selecting best parameters for certain model, Example in caret[49]. The equivalent in **Python** is included in Scikit Learn[50].
- The best test is the one made by you, suited to your data and needs. Try different models and analyze the tradeoff between time consumption and any accuracy metric.

These re-sampling techniques could be among the powerful tools behind the sites like stackoverflow.com or collaborative open-source software. To have many opinions to produce a less-biased solution.

But each opinion has to be reliable, imagine asking for a medical diagnostic to different doctors.

4.1.8 Further reading

- Tutorial: Cross validation for predictive analytics using R[51]
- Tutorial by Max Kahn (caret's creator): Comparing Different Species of Cross-Validation[52]
- The cross-validation approach can also be applied to time dependant models, check the other chapter: Out-of-time Validation.

---

[49]https://topepo.github.io/caret/model-training-and-tuning.html

[50]http://scikit-learn.org/stable/modules/cross_validation.html

[51]http://www.milanor.net/blog/cross-validation-for-predictive-analytics-using-r

[52]http : / / appliedpredictivemodeling . com / blog / 2014 / 11 / 27 / vpuig01pqbklmi72b8lcl3ij5hj2qm

4.2 Out-of-Time Validation

4.2.1 What's this about?

Once we've built a predictive model, how sure we are it captured general patterns and not just the data it has seen (overfitting)?.

Will it perform well when it is on production / running live? What is the expected error?

4.2.2 What sort of data?

If it's generated over time and -let's say- every day we have new cases like *"page visits on a website"*, or *"new patients arriving at a medical center"*, one strong validation is the **Out-Of-Time** approach.

4.2.3 Out-Of-Time Validation Example

How to?

Imagine we are building the model on **Jan-01**, then to build the model we use all the data **before Oct-31**. Between these two dates, there are 2 months.

When predicting a **binary/two class variable** (or multi-class), it's quite straightforward: with the model we've built -with data <= **Oct-31**- we score the data on that exact day, and then we measure how the users/patients/persons/cases evolved during those two months.

Since the output of a binary model should be a number indicating the likelihood for each case to belong to a particular class (Scoring Data chapter), we test what the **model "*said*" on Oct-31 against what it actually happened on "Jan-01"**.

Following **validation workflow** may be helpful when building a predictive model involving time.

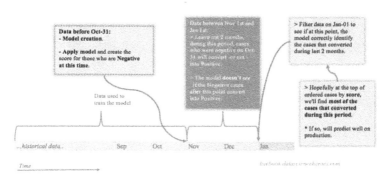

Figure 83: A validation workflow for time dependant problems

Enlarge image.[53]

---

[53]http://datascienceheroes.com/img/blog/model_validation_workflow.png

4.2.4   Using Gain and Lift Analysis

This analysis explained in another chapter (Gain & Lift) and it can be used following the out-of-time validation.

Keeping only with those cases that were **negative** on `Oct-31`, we get the `score` returned by the model on that date, and the `target` variable is the value that those cases had on `Jan-1`.

4.2.5   How about a numerical target variable?

Now the common sense and business need is more present. A numerical outcome can take any value, it can increase or decrease through time, so we may have to consider these two scenarios to help us thinking what we consider success. This is the case of linear regression.

Example scenario: We measure some web app usage (like the home-banking), the standard thing is as the days pass, the users use it more.

Examples:

- Predicting the concentration of a certain substance in the blood.
- Predicting page visits.
- Time series analysis.

We also have in these cases the difference between: **"what was ex-pected" vs. "what it is"**.

This difference can take any number. This is the error or residuals.

User ID	Page visits on Oct-31	Prediction (on Oct-31) for Jan-01	Real value on Jan-01	Error / Difference / Residuals
1	23	50	63	-13
2	1	66	8	58
3	94	52	43	9
4	34	60	102	-42
...	...	...	...	and so on...

Figure 84: Prediction and error analysis

If the model is good, this error should be **white noise**, more info in *"Time series analysis and regression"* section inside (Wikipedia 2017d). It follows a normal curve when mainly there are some logical properties:

- The error should be **around 0** -*the model must tend its error to 0*-.
- The standard deviation from this error **must be finite** -to avoid unpredictable outliers-.
- There has to be no correlation between the errors.
- **Normal distribution**: expect the majority of errors around 0, having the biggest ones in a **smaller proportion** as the error increases -likelihood of finding bigger errors decreases exponentially-

.

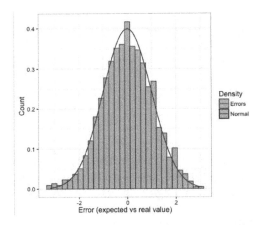

Figure 85: A nice error curve (normal distribution)

4.2.6 Final thoughts

- **Out-of-Time Validation** is a powerful validation tool to simulate the running of the model on production with data that may **not need to depend on sampling**.

- The **error analysis** is a big chapter in data science. Time to go to next chapter which will try to cover key-concepts on this: Knowing the error.

Data Science Live Book

4.3 Gain and Lift Analysis

4.3.1 What is this about?

Both metrics are extremely useful to validate the predictive model
(binary outcome) quality. More info about scoring data

Make sure we have the latest `funModeling` version ($>=$ 1.3).

```
# Loading funModeling
library(funModeling)
```

```
# Create a GLM model
fit_glm = glm(has_heart_disease ~ age + oldpeak,
  data = heart_disease, family = binomial)
```

```
# Get the scores/probabilities for each row
heart_disease$score = predict(fit_glm,
  newdata = heart_disease, type = "response")
```

```
# Plot the gain and lift curve
gain_lift(data = heart_disease, score = "score",
  target = "has_heart_disease")
```

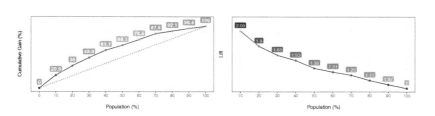

Figure 86: Gain and lift curves

```
##     Population   Gain Lift Score.Point
## 1           10  20.86 2.09   0.8185793
```

```
## 2              20  35.97 1.80    0.6967124
## 3              30  48.92 1.63    0.5657817
## 4              40  61.15 1.53    0.4901940
## 5              50  69.06 1.38    0.4033640
## 6              60  78.42 1.31    0.3344170
## 7              70  87.77 1.25    0.2939878
## 8              80  92.09 1.15    0.2473671
## 9              90  96.40 1.07    0.1980453
## 10            100 100.00 1.00    0.1195511
```

4.3.2   How to interpret it?

First, each case is ordered according to the likelihood of being the less representative class, aka, score value.

Then `Gain` column accumulates the positive class, for each 10% of rows - `Population` column.

So for the first row, it can be read as:

"The first 10 percent of the population, ordered by score, collects 20.86% of total positive cases"

For example, if we are sending emails based on this model, and we have a budget to reach only **20%** of our users, how many responses we should expect to get? **Answer: 35.97%**

4.3.3   What about not using a model?

If we **don't use a model**, and we select randomly 20%, how many users do we have to reach? Well, 20%. That is the meaning of the **dashed line**, which starts at 0% and ends at 100%. Hopefully, with the predictive model we'll beat the randomness.

The **Lift** column represents the ratio, between the `Gain` and the *gain by chance*. Taking as an example the Population=20%, the model is **1.8 times better** than randomness.

4.3.3.1 Using the cut point ✂

What value of the score reaches 30% of the population? Answer: `0.56`

The cut point allows us to segment the data.

4.3.3.2 Comparing models

In a good model, the gain will reach the 100% "at the beginning" of the population, representing that it separates the classes.

When comparing models, a quick metric is to see if the gain at the beginning of the population (10-30%) is higher.

As a result, the model with a higher gain at the beginning will have captured more information from data.

Let's illustrate it...

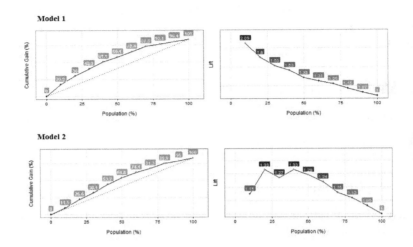

Figure 87: Comparing the gain and lift curves for two models

Enlarge image.[54]

Cumulative Gain Analysis: Model 1 reaches the ~20% of positive cases around the 10% of the population, while model 2 reaches a similar proportion approaching the 20% of the population. *Model 1 is better.*

Lift analysis: Same as before, but also it is suspicious that not every lift number follow a decreasing pattern. Maybe the model is not ordering the first percentiles of the population. Same ordering concepts as seen in Profiling target using cross_plot chapter.

---

[54]http://datascienceheroes.com/img/blog/model_comparison.png

4.4 Scoring Data

4.4.1 The intuition behind

Events can occur, or not... although we don't have *tomorrow's news-paper* , we can make a good guess about how is it going to be.

The future is undoubtedly attached to *uncertainty*, and this uncertainty can be estimated.

4.4.1.1 And there are differents targets...

For now, this book will cover the classical: `Yes/No` target -also known as binary or multiclass prediction.

So, this estimation is the *value of truth* of an event to happen, therefore a probabilistic value between 0 and 1.

4.4.1.2 Two-label vs. multi-label outcome

Please note this chapter is written for a binary outcome (two-label outcome), but **multi-label** target can be seen as a general approach of a binary class.

For example, having a target with 4 different values, there can be 4 models that predict the likelihood of belonging to particular class, or not. And then a higher model which takes the results of those 4 models and predict the final class.

4.4.1.3 Say what? 😳

Some examples: - Is this client going to buy this product? - Is this patient going to get better? - Is certain event going to happen in the next few weeks?

The answers to these last questions are True or False, but **the essence is to have a score**, or a number indicating the likelihood of a certain event to happen.

4.4.1.4 But we need more control. . .

Many machine learning resources show the simplified version -which is good to start- getting the final class as an output. Let's say:

Simplified approach:

- Question: *Is this person going to have a heart disease?*

- Answer: "No"

But there is something else before the "Yes/No" answer, and this is the score:

- Question: *What is the likelihood for this person of having heart disease?*
- Answer: "25%"

So first we get the score, and then according to our needs we set the **cut point**. And this is **really** important.

4.4.2 Let see an example

id	x1	x2	x3	target
1	2.3	2.3	1.5	yes
2	2.1	2.4	0.2	no
3	2.6	1.6	1.0	no
4	2.3	2.5	0.7	yes
5	2.5	2.0	0.4	yes
6	2.0	2.4	0.5	no
7	1.9	2.4	0.1	no
8	1.7	2.4	0.1	no
9	1.9	1.9	0.2	no
10	2.4	2.0	0.9	no
11	2.4	1.7	1.3	yes
12	2.1	2.3	0.3	no
13	2.4	2.3	0.3	no
14	1.9	2.0	0.2	no
15	1.7	2.4	0.6	yes

Figure 88: Simple dataset example

Example table showing the following

- `id`=identity

259

- **x1,x2** and **x3** input variables
- **target**=variable to predict

id	target	score
1	yes	0.8
2	no	0.2
3	no	0.14
4	yes	0.98
5	yes	0.4
6	no	0.23
7	no	0.21
8	no	0.87
9	no	0.11
10	no	0.5
11	yes	0.89
12	no	0.11
13	no	0.34
14	no	0.23
15	yes	0.85

Figure 89: Getting the score (predictive model output)

Forgetting about input variables... After the creation of the predictive model, like a random forest, we are interested in the **scores**. Even though our final goal is to deliver a **yes/no** predicted variable.

For example, the following 2 sentences express the same: *The likelihood of being **yes** is 0.8 <=> The probability of being **no** is 0.2*

Maybe it is understood, but the score usually refers to the less representative class: **yes**.

☝ R Syntax *-skip it if you don't want to see code-*

Following sentence will return the score:

```
score = predict(randomForestModel, data, type = "prob")[,
```

2]

Please note for other models this syntax may vary a little, but the concept **will remain the same**. Even for other languages.

Where `prob` indicates we want the probabilities (or scores).

The `predict` function + `type="prob"` parameter returns a matrix of 15 rows and 2 columns: the 1st indicates the likelihood of being **no** while the 2nd one shows the same for class **yes**.

Since target variable can be **no** or **yes**, the [, 2] return the likelihood of being -in this case- **yes** (which is the complement of the **no** likelihood).

4.4.3 It's all about the cut point ✎

Id	target	score (ordered)
4	yes	0.98
11	yes	0.89
8	no	0.87
15	yes	0.85
1	yes	0.8
10	no	0.5
5	yes	0.4
13	no	0.34
6	no	0.23
14	no	0.23
7	no	0.21
2	no	0.2
3	no	0.14
9	no	0.11
12	no	0.11

Figure 90: Cases ordered by highest score

Now the table is ordered by descending score.

261

This is meant to see how to extract the final class having by default the cut point in `0.5`. Tweaking the cut point will lead to a better classification.

> Accuracy metrics or the confusion matrix are always attached to a certain cut point value.

After assigning the cut point, we can see the classification results getting the famous:

- ✅**True Positive** (TP): It's *true*, that the classification is *positive*, or, "the model hit correctly the positive (**yes**) class".
- ✅**True Negative** (TN): Same as before, but with negative class (**no**).
- ❌**False Positive** (FP): It's *false*, that the classification is *positive*, or, "the model missed, it predicted **yes** but the result was **no**
- ❌**False Negative** (FN): Same as before, but with negative class, "the model predicted negative, but it was positive", or, "the model predicted **no**, but the class was **yes**"

Id	target	score (ordered)	predicted label (cutpoint @ 0.5)	Accuracy
4	yes	0.98	yes	TP
11	yes	0.89	yes	TP
8	no	0.87	yes	FP
15	yes	0.85	yes	TP
1	yes	0.8	yes	TP
10	no	0.5	yes	FP
5	yes	0.4	no	FN
13	no	0.34	no	TN
6	no	0.23	no	TN
14	no	0.23	no	TN
7	no	0.21	no	TN
2	no	0.2	no	TN
3	no	0.14	no	TN
9	no	0.11	no	TN
12	no	0.11	no	TN

Figure 91: Assigning the predicted label (cutoff=0.5)

4.4.4   The best and the worst scenario

Just like Zen does, the analysis of the extremes will help to find the middle point.

The best scenario is when **TP** and **TN** rates are 100%. That means the model correctly predicts all the **yes** and all the **no**; *(as a result, FP and FN rates are 0%).*

But wait ! If we find a perfect classification, probably it's because of overfitting!

The worst scenario -the opposite to last example- is when **FP** and **FN** rates are 100%. Not even randomness can achieve such an awful scenario.

Why? If the classes are balanced, 50/50, flipping a coin will assert around half of the results. This is the common baseline to test if the model is better than randomness.

In the example provided, class distribution is 5 for **yes**, and 10 for **no**; so: **33,3%** (5/15) is **yes**.

4.4.5   Comparing classifiers

4.4.5.1   Comparing classification results

? Trivia: Is a model which correcltly predict this 33.3% (TP rate=100%) a good one?

Answer: It depends on how many 'yes', the model predicted.

A classifier that always predicts **yes**, will have a TP of 100%, but is absolutely useless since lots of **yes** will be actually **no**. As a matter of fact, FP rate will be high.

4.4.5.2 Comparing ordering label based on score

A classifier must be trustful, and this is what **ROC** curves measures when plotting the TP vs FP rates. The higher the proportion of TP over FP, the higher the Area Under Roc Curve (AUC) is.

The intuition behind ROC curve is to get an **sanity measure** regarding the **score**: how well it orders the label. Ideally, all the positive labels must be at the top, and the negative ones at the bottom.

id	target	model 1 (good)
4	yes	0.98
11	yes	0.89
8	no	0.87
15	yes	0.85
1	yes	0.8
10	no	0.5
5	yes	0.4
13	no	0.34
6	no	0.23
14	no	0.23
7	no	0.21
2	no	0.2
3	no	0.14
9	no	0.11
12	no	0.11

id	target	model 2 (bad)
14	no	0.99
8	no	0.87
15	yes	0.85
2	no	0.8
10	no	0.7
11	yes	0.5
9	no	0.5
5	yes	0.4
7	no	0.36
13	no	0.34
4	yes	0.3
1	yes	0.3
3	no	0.3
6	no	0.23
12	no	0.11

Figure 92: Comparing two predictive model scores

`model 1` will have a higher AUC than `model 2`.

Wikipedia has an extensive and good article on this: https://en. wikipedia.org/wiki/Receiver_operating_characteristic

There is the comparission of 4 models, given a cutpoint of 0.5:

264

A			B			C			C'		
TP=63	FN=37	100	TP=77	FN=23	100	TP=24	FN=76	100	TP=76	FN=24	100
FP=28	TN=72	100	FP=77	TN=23	100	FP=88	TN=12	100	FP=12	TN=88	100
91	109	200	154	46	200	112	88	200	88	112	200
TPR = 0.63			TPR = 0.77			TPR = 0.24			TPR = 0.76		
FPR = 0.28			FPR = 0.77			FPR = 0.88			FPR = 0.12		
PPV = 0.69			PPV = 0.50			PPV = 0.21			PPV = 0.86		
F1 = 0.66			F1 = 0.61			F1 = 0.22			F1 = 0.81		
ACC = 0.68			ACC = 0.50			ACC = 0.18			ACC = 0.82		

Figure 93: Comparing four predictive models

4.4.6 Hands on R!

We'll be analyzing three scenarios based on different cut-points.

```
# install.packages('rpivotTable') rpivotTable: it creates
# a pivot table dinamically, it also supports plots, more
# info at:
# https://github.com/smartinsightsfromdata/rpivotTable

library(rpivotTable)

## reading the data
data = read.delim(file = "https://goo.gl/ac5AkG",
  sep = "\t", header = T, stringsAsFactors = F)
```

4.4.6.1 Scenario 1: cut point @ 0.5

Classical confusion matrix, indicating how many cases fall in the intersection of real vs predicted value:

```
data$predicted_target = ifelse(data$score >= 0.5, "yes",
  "no")

rpivotTable(data = data, rows = "predicted_target",
  cols = "target", aggregatorName = "Count",
  rendererName = "Table", width = "100%",
  height = "400px")
```

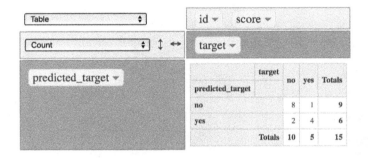

Figure 94: Confusion matrix (metric: count)

Another view, now each column sums **100%**. Good to answer the following questions:

```
rpivotTable(data = data,
  rows = "predicted_target",
  cols = "target",
  aggregatorName = "Count as Fraction of Columns",
  rendererName = "Table",
  width = "100%", height = "400px")
```

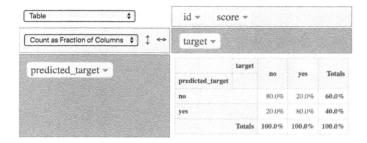

Figure 95: Confusion matrix (cutpoint at 0.5)

- *What is the percentage of real **yes** values captured by the model?*
  Answer: 80% Also known as **Precision** (PPV)
- *What is the percentage of **yes** thrown by the model? 40%.*

So, from the last two sentences:

The model throws 4 out of 10 predictions as yes, and from this segment -the yes- it hits 80%.

Another view: The model correctly hits 3 cases for each 10 **yes** predictions *(0.4/0.8=3.2, or 3, rounding down).*

Note: The last way of analysis can be found when building an association rules (market basket analysis), and a decision tree model.

4.4.6.2   Scenario 2: cut point @ 0.4

Time to change the cut point to 0.4, so the amount of **yes** will be higher:

```
data$predicted_target = ifelse(data$score >= 0.4, "yes",
  "no")

rpivotTable(data = data,
```

267

```
rows = "predicted_target",
cols = "target",
aggregatorName = "Count as Fraction of Columns",
rendererName = "Table",
width = "100%", height = "400px")
```

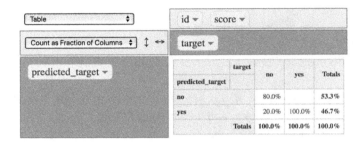

Figure 96: Confusion matrix (cutpoint at 0.4)

Now the model captures 100% of yes (TP), so the total amount of yes produced by the model increased to 46.7%, but at no cost since the *TN and FP remained the same* :thumbsup:.

4.4.6.3 Scenario 3: cut point @ 0.8

Want to decrease the FP rate? Set the cut point to a higher value, for example: 0.8, which will cause the yes produced by the model decreases:

```
data$predicted_target = ifelse(data$score >= 0.8, "yes",
  "no")

rpivotTable(data = data,
  rows = "predicted_target",
  cols = "target",
```

```
aggregatorName = "Count as Fraction of Columns",
rendererName = "Table",
width = "100%", height = "400px")
```

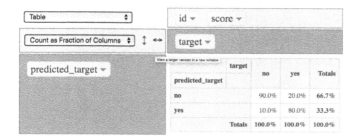

Figure 97: Confusion matrix (cutpoint at 0.8)

Now the FP rate decreased to 10% (from 20%), and the model still captures the 80% of TP which is the same rate as the one obtained with a cut point of 0.5 :thumbsup:.

Decreasing the cut point to 0.8 improved the model at no cost.

4.4.7   Conclusions

- This chapter has focused on the essence of predicting a binary variable: To produce a score or likelihood number which **orders** the target variable.

- A predictive model maps the input with the output.

- There is not a unique and best **cut point value**, it relies on the project needs, and is constrained by the rate of `False Positive` and `False Negative` we can accept.

This book addresses general aspects on model performance in Knowing the error.

Data Science Live Book

5 APPENDIX

Complementary reading.

5.1 The magic of percentiles

Percentile is such a crucial concept in data analysis that we are going to cover it extensively in this book. It considers each observation with respect to others. An isolated number may not be meaningful, but when it is compared with others the distribution concept appears.

Percentiles are used in profiling as well as evaluating the performance of a predictive model.

Step 1	Step 2	Step 3	Step 4	
original variable	ordered variable	*position ordered variable*	**position in percent ordered variable (percentile)**	
32	29	1	8%	**Case 1:** Which is the median? (percentile 50th). The highest value for the 1st 50% of the ordered variable.
54	32	2	17%	**Answer:** 54 *(see note 1)*
74	38	3	25%	
99	41	4	33%	
38	53	5	42%	
55	54	6	50%	**Case 2:** What is the percentile 90th? (or what is the value at 90th position?)
29	55	7	58%	
41	74	8	67%	It cannot be computed directly, we need to interpolate between the 83th and 92nd percentile.
134	93	9	75%	
53	99	10	83%	
209	134	11	92%	**Answer:** ~ 130 *(see note 1)*
93	209	12	100%	

Note 1: The results may vary according to the interpolation method. There are many of them.

In **R** the default **quantile** function retrieves the values 54.5 and 130.5 for cases 1 and 2 respectively. *In Microsoft Excel these values are slightly different.*

http://livebook.datascienceheroes.com/

More info: help("quantile")

Figure 98: How to calculate percentiles

The dataset, an advice before continue:

This contains many indicators regarding world development. Regardless the profiling example, the idea is to provide a ready-to-use table for sociologists, researchers, etc. interested in analyzing this kind of data.

The original data source is: http://databank.worldbank.org. There you will find a data dictionary that explains all the variables.

In this section we'll be using a table which is already prepared for analysis. The complete step-by-step data preparation is in Profiling chapter.

Any indicator meaning can be checked in data.worldbank.org. For example, if we want to know what `EN.POP.SLUM.UR.ZS` means, then we type: http://data.worldbank.org/indicator/EN.POP.SLUM.UR.ZS

5.1.1 How to calculate percentiles

There are several methods to get the percentile. Based on interpolations, the easiest way is to order the variable ascendantly, selecting the percentile we want (for example, 75%), and then observing *what is the maximum value if we want to choose the 75% of the ordered population.*

Now we are going to use the technique of keeping a small sample so that we can have maximum control over *what is going on* behind the calculus.

We retain the random 10 countries and print the vector of `rural_poverty_headcount` which is the variable we are going to use.

```
library(dplyr)

data_world_wide =
  read.delim(file="https://goo.gl/NNYhCW",
             header = T
             )

data_sample = filter(data_world_wide, Country.Name %in%
  c("Kazakhstan", "Zambia", "Mauritania", "Malaysia",
    "Sao Tome and Principe", "Colombia", "Haiti",
    "Fiji", "Sierra Leone", "Morocco")) %>%
  arrange(rural_poverty_headcount)

select(data_sample, Country.Name,
  rural_poverty_headcount)
```

```
##              Country.Name rural_poverty_headcount
## 1              Malaysia                        1.6
## 2            Kazakhstan                        4.4
## 3               Morocco                       14.4
## 4              Colombia                       40.3
## 5                  Fiji                       44.0
## 6            Mauritania                       59.4
## 7  Sao Tome and Principe                      59.4
## 8          Sierra Leone                       66.1
## 9                 Haiti                       74.9
## 10                Zambia                       77.9
```

Please note that the vector is ordered only for didactic purposes. *As we said in the Profiling chapter, our eyes like order.*

Now we apply the `quantile` function on `rural_poverty_headcount` variable (the percentage of the rural population living below the national poverty lines):

```
quantile(data_sample$rural_poverty_headcount)
```

```
##     0%    25%    50%    75%   100%
##  1.600 20.875 51.700 64.425 77.900
```

Analysis

- **Percentile 50%**: 50% of the countries (five of them) have a `rural_poverty_headcount` below `51.7` We can check this in the last table: these countries are: Fiji, Colombia, Morocco, Kazakhstan, and Malaysia.
- **Percentile 25%**: 25% of the countries are below 20.87. Here we can see an interpolation because 25% represents ~2.5 countries. If we use this value to filter the countries, then we'll get three countries: Morocco, Kazakhstan, and Malaysia.

More information about the different types of quantiles and their interpolations: `help("quantile")`.

5.1.1.1 Getting semantical descriptions

From the last example we can state that:

- *"Half of the countries have as much as 51.7% of rural poverty"*
- *"Three-quarters of the countries have a maximum of 64.4% regarding its rural poverty"* (based on the countries ordered ascendantly).

We can also think of **using the opposite**:

- *"A quarter of the countries that exhibit the highest rural poverty values have a percentage of at least 64.4%."*

5.1.2 Calculating custom quantiles

Typically, we want to calculate certain quantiles. The example variable will be the `gini_index`

What is the Gini index?

It is a measure of income or wealth inequality.

- A Gini coefficient of **zero** expresses **perfect equality** where all values are the same (for example, where everyone has the same income).
- A Gini coefficient of **1** (or 100%) expresses **maximal inequality** among values (e.g., for a large number of people, where only one person has all the income or consumption while all others have none, the Gini coefficient will be very nearly one).

Source: https://en.wikipedia.org/wiki/Gini_coefficient

Example in R:

If we want to get the 20, 40, 60, and 80th quantiles of the Gini index variable, we use again the `quantile` function.

The `na.rm=TRUE` parameter is necessary if we have empty values like in this case:

```
# We also can get multiple quantiles at once
p_custom = quantile(data_world_wide$gini_index,
  probs = c(0.2, 0.4, 0.6, 0.8), na.rm = TRUE)
p_custom
```

```
##     20%    40%    60%    80%
## 31.624 35.244 41.076 46.148
```

5.1.3 Indicating where most of the values are

In descriptive statistics, we want to describe the population in general terms. We can speak about ranges using two percentiles. Let's take the percentiles 10 and 90th to describe 80% of the population.

The poverty ranges from 0.075% to 54.4% in 80% of the countries. (80% because we did 90th–10th, focusing on the middle of the population.)

If we consider the 80% as the majority of the population, then we could say: *"Normally (or in general terms), poverty goes from 0.07% to 54.4%"*. This is a semantical description.

We looked at 80% of the population, which seems a good number to describe where most of the cases are. We also could have used the 90% range (percentile 95th - 0.5th).

5.1.3.1 Is percentile related to quartile?

Quartile is a formal name for the 25, 50, and 75th percentiles (quarters or 'Q'). If we look at the 50% of the population, we need to subtract the

3rd quartile (or 75th percentile) from the 1st quartile (25th percentile) to get where 50% of data are concentrated, also known as the **interquartile range** or IQR.

Percentile vs. quantile vs. quartile

```
0 quartile = 0 quantile = 0 percentile
1 quartile = 0.25 quantile = 25 percentile
2 quartile = .5 quantile = 50 percentile (median)
3 quartile = .75 quantile = 75 percentile
4 quartile = 1 quantile = 100 percentile
```

Credits: (stats.stackexchange.com 2017b).

5.1.4 Visualizing quantiles

Plotting a histogram alongisde the places where each percentile is can help us understand the concept:

```
quantiles_var =
  quantile(data_world_wide$poverty_headcount_1.9,
          c(0.25, 0.5, 0.75),
          na.rm = T
          )

df_p = data.frame(value=quantiles_var,
                  quantile=c("25th", "50th", "75th")
                  )

library(ggplot2)
ggplot(data_world_wide, aes(poverty_headcount_1.9)) +
  geom_histogram() +
  geom_vline(data=df_p,
            aes(xintercept=value,
```

```
            colour = quantile),
        show.legend = TRUE,
        linetype="dashed"
        ) +
theme_light()
```

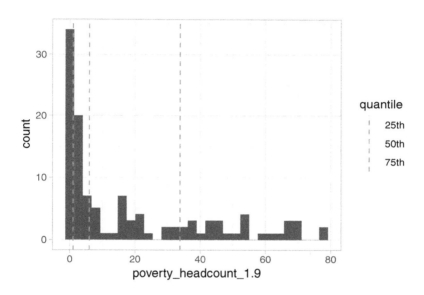

Figure 99: Visualizing quantiles

If we sum all the gray bars before the 25th percentile, then it will be around the height of the gray bars sum after the 75th percentile.

In the last plot, the IQR appears between the first and the last dashed lines and contains 50% of the population.

5.1.5 Rank and top/bottom '*X%*' concepts

The ranking concept is the same as the one seen in competitions. It allows us to answer *what is the country with the highest rate in variable pop_living_slums?*

We'll use the `dense_rank` function from the `ggplot2` package. It assigns the position (rank) to each country, but we need them in reverse order; that is, we assign the `rank = 1` to the highest value.

Now the variable will be: *Population living in slums is the proportion of the urban population living in slum households. A slum household is defined as a group of individuals living under the same roof and lacking one or more of the following conditions: access to improved water, access to improved sanitation, sufficient living area, and durability of housing.*

The question to answer: *What are the top six countries with the highest rates of people living in slums?*

```
# Creating rank variable
data_world_wide$rank_pop_living_slums =
  dense_rank(-data_world_wide$pop_living_slums)

# Ordering data by rank
data_world_wide = arrange(data_world_wide,
  rank_pop_living_slums)

# Printing the first six results
select(data_world_wide, Country.Name,
  rank_pop_living_slums) %>% head(.)
```

```
##                   Country.Name rank_pop_living_slums
## 1                  South Sudan                     1
## 2 Central African Republic                         2
## 3                       Sudan                      3
```

```
## 4                      Chad                      4
## 5      Sao Tome and Principe                      5
## 6              Guinea-Bissau                       6
```

We can also ask: *In which position is Ecuador?*

```
filter(data_world_wide, Country.Name == "Ecuador") %>%
  select(rank_pop_living_slums)
```

```
##    rank_pop_living_slums
## 1                     57
```

5.1.5.0.1   Top and bottom 'X%' concepts

Other questions that we may be interested in answering: *What is the value for which I get the top 10% of lowest values?*

The 10th percentile is the answer:

```
quantile(data_world_wide$pop_living_slums, probs = 0.1,
  na.rm = T)
```

```
##   10%
## 12.5
```

Working on the opposite: *What is the value for which I get the bottom 10% of highest values?*

The 90th percentile is the answer, we can filter all the cases above this value:

```
quantile(data_world_wide$pop_living_slums, probs = 0.9,
  na.rm = T)
```

```
##   90%
## 75.2
```

5.1.6 Percentile in scoring data

There are two chapters that use this concept:

- Data Scoring
- Gain and Lift Analysis

The basic idea is to develop a predictive model that predicts a binary variable (**yes**/**no**). Suppose we need to score new cases, for example, to use in a marketing campaign. The question to answer is:

What is the score value to suggest to sales people in order to capture 50% of potential new sales? The answer comes from a combination of percentile analysis on the scoring value plus the cumulative analysis of the current target.

Model 1

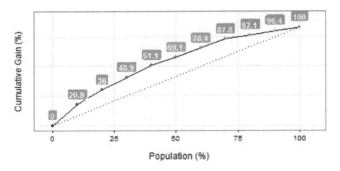

Figure 100: Gain and lift curves (model performance)

5.1.6.1 Case study: distribution of wealth

The distribution of wealth is similar to the Gini index and is focused on inequality. It measures owner assets (which is different from income), making the comparison across countries more even to what people can

280

acquire according to the place where they live. For a better definition, please go to the *Wikipedia* article and *Global Wealth Report 2013*. Refs. (Wikipedia 2017a) and (Suisse 2013) respectively.

Quoting *Wikipedia* (Ref. (Wikipedia 2017a)):

> half of the world's wealth belongs to the top 1% of the population;

> the top 10% of adults hold 85% while the bottom 90% hold the remaining 15% of the world's total wealth; and

> the top 30% of adults hold 97% of the total wealth.

Just as we did before, from the third sentence we can state that: *"3% of total wealth is distributed to 70% of adults."*

The metrics `top 10%` and `top 30%` are the quantiles `0.1` and `0.3`. Wealth is the numeric variable.

5.2   funModeling quick-start

This package contains a set of functions related to exploratory data analysis, data preparation, and model performance. It is used by people coming from business, research, and teaching (professors and students).

`funModeling` is intimately related to this book, in the sense that most of its functionality is used to explain different topics addressed by the book.

5.2.1 Opening the black-box

Some functions have in-line comments so the user can open the black-box and learn how it was developed, or to tune or improve any of them.

All the functions are well documented, explaining all the parameters with the help of many short examples. R documentation can be accessed by: `help("name_of_the_function")`.

Important changes from latest version 1.6.7, (relevant only if you were using previous versions):

From the latest version, 1.6.7 (Jan 21-2018), the parameters `str_input`, `str_target` and `str_score` will be renamed to `input`, `target` and `score` respectively. The functionality remains the same. If you were using these parameters names on production, they will be still working until next release. this means that for now, you can use for example `str_input` or `input`.

The other importat change was in `discretize_get_bins`, which is detailed later in this document.

5.2.1.1 About this quick-start

This quick-start is focused only on the functions. All explanations around them, and the how and when to use them, can be accessed by following the "***Read more here.***" links below each section, which redirect you to the book.

Below there are most of the `funModeling` functions divided by category.

5.2.2 Exploratory data analysis

5.2.2.1 df_status: Dataset health status

Use case: analyze the zeros, missing values (NA), infinity, data type, and number of unique values for a given dataset.

```
library(funModeling)
```

```
df_status(heart_disease)
```

```
##                      variable q_zeros p_zeros q_na p_na
## 1                         age       0    0.00    0 0.00
## 2                      gender       0    0.00    0 0.00
## 3                  chest_pain       0    0.00    0 0.00
## 4       resting_blood_pressure       0    0.00    0 0.00
## 5          serum_cholestoral       0    0.00    0 0.00
## 6          fasting_blood_sugar     258   85.15    0 0.00
## 7              resting_electro     151   49.83    0 0.00
## 8              max_heart_rate       0    0.00    0 0.00
## 9                  exer_angina     204   67.33    0 0.00
## 10                     oldpeak      99   32.67    0 0.00
## 11                       slope       0    0.00    0 0.00
## 12          num_vessels_flour     176   58.09    4 1.32
## 13                        thal       0    0.00    2 0.66
## 14      heart_disease_severity     164   54.13    0 0.00
## 15                 exter_angina     204   67.33    0 0.00
## 16           has_heart_disease       0    0.00    0 0.00
##      q_inf p_inf     type unique
## 1        0     0  integer     41
## 2        0     0   factor      2
## 3        0     0   factor      4
## 4        0     0  integer     50
## 5        0     0  integer    152
```

283

```
## 6       0     0  factor     2
## 7       0     0  factor     3
## 8       0     0 integer    91
## 9       0     0 integer     2
## 10      0     0 numeric    40
## 11      0     0 integer     3
## 12      0     0 integer     4
## 13      0     0  factor     3
## 14      0     0 integer     5
## 15      0     0  factor     2
## 16      0     0  factor     2
```

[🔍Read more here.]

5.2.2.2 plot_num: Plotting distributions for numerical variables

Plots only numeric variables.

```
plot_num(heart_disease)
```

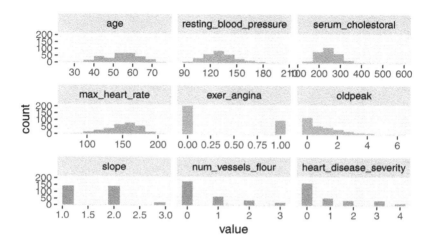

Figure 101: plot num: visualizing numerical variables

Notes:

- `bins`: Sets the number of bins (10 by default).
- `path_out` indicates the path directory; if it has a value, then the plot is exported in jpeg. To save in current directory path must be dot: "."

[⚲Read more here.]

5.2.2.3 profiling_num: Calculating several statistics for numerical variables

Retrieves several statistics for numerical variables.

```
profiling_num(heart_disease)
```

```
##                 variable   mean std_dev variation_coef
## 1                   age  54.44    9.04           0.17
```

285

```
## 2   resting_blood_pressure 131.69   17.60          0.13
## 3       serum_cholestoral 246.69   51.78          0.21
## 4          max_heart_rate 149.61   22.88          0.15
## 5              exer_angina   0.33    0.47          1.44
## 6                  oldpeak   1.04    1.16          1.12
## 7                    slope   1.60    0.62          0.38
## 8         num_vessels_flour   0.67    0.94          1.39
## 9  heart_disease_severity   0.94    1.23          1.31
##    p_01 p_05 p_25 p_50  p_75  p_95  p_99 skewness
## 1    35   40   48 56.0  61.0  68.0  71.0    -0.21
## 2   100  108  120 130.0 140.0 160.0 180.0     0.70
## 3   149  175  211 241.0 275.0 326.9 406.7     1.13
## 4    95  108  134 153.0 166.0 181.9 192.0    -0.53
## 5     0    0    0  0.0   1.0   1.0   1.0     0.74
## 6     0    0    0  0.8   1.6   3.4   4.2     1.26
## 7     1    1    1  2.0   2.0   3.0   3.0     0.51
## 8     0    0    0  0.0   1.0   3.0   3.0     1.18
## 9     0    0    0  0.0   2.0   3.0   4.0     1.05
##    kurtosis  iqr      range_98        range_80
## 1       2.5 13.0     [35, 71]        [42, 66]
## 2       3.8 20.0    [100, 180]      [110, 152]
## 3       7.4 64.0  [149, 406.74] [188.8, 308.8]
## 4       2.9 32.5 [95.02, 191.96]   [116, 176.6]
## 5       1.5  1.0       [0, 1]          [0, 1]
## 6       4.5  1.6     [0, 4.2]        [0, 2.8]
## 7       2.4  1.0       [1, 3]          [1, 2]
## 8       3.2  1.0       [0, 3]          [0, 2]
## 9       2.8  2.0       [0, 4]          [0, 3]
```

Note:

- plot_num and profiling_num automatically exclude non-numeric variables

[✏Read more here.]

5.2.2.4 freq: Getting frequency distributions for categoric variables

```
library(dplyr)
```

```
# Select only two variables for this example
heart_disease_2 = heart_disease %>% select(chest_pain,
   thal)
```

```
# Frequency distribution
freq(heart_disease_2)
```

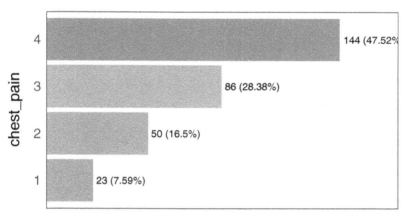

Figure 102: freq: visualizing categorical variables

```
##    chest_pain frequency percentage cumulative_perc
## 1           4       144       47.5              48
## 2           3        86       28.4              76
```

287

| ## 3 | 2 | 50 | 16.5 | 92 |
| ## 4 | 1 | 23 | 7.6 | 100 |

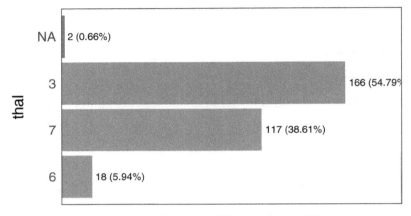

Frequency / (Percentage %)

Figure 103: freq: visualizing categorical variables

```
##     thal frequency percentage cumulative_perc
## 1    3        166      54.79              55
## 2    7        117      38.61              93
## 3    6         18       5.94              99
## 4 <NA>         2        0.66             100
```

```
## [1] "Variables processed: chest_pain, thal"
```

Notes:

- freq only processes factor and character, excluding non-categorical variables.
- It returns the distribution table as a data frame.
- If input is empty, then it runs for all categorical variables.
- path_out indicates the path directory; if it has a value, then the plot is exported in jpeg. To save in current directory path must

be dot: "."

- `na.rm` indicates if `NA` values should be excluded (`FALSE` by default).

[✎Read more here.]

5.2.3 Correlations

5.2.3.1 `correlation_table`: Calculates R statistic

Retrieves R metric (or Pearson coefficient) for all numeric variables, skipping the categoric ones.

```
correlation_table(heart_disease, "has_heart_disease")
```

```
##                    Variable has_heart_disease
## 1        has_heart_disease              1.00
## 2 heart_disease_severity              0.83
## 3       num_vessels_flour              0.46
## 4                  oldpeak              0.42
## 5                    slope              0.34
## 6                      age              0.23
## 7 resting_blood_pressure              0.15
## 8       serum_cholestoral              0.08
## 9          max_heart_rate             -0.42
```

Notes:

- Only numeric variables are analyzed. Target variable must be numeric.
- If target is categorical, then it will be converted to numeric.

[✎Read more here.]

5.2.3.2 `var_rank_info`: Correlation based on information theory

Calculates correlation based on several information theory metrics between all variables in a data frame and a target variable.

`var_rank_info(heart_disease, "has_heart_disease")`

```
##                             var  en     mi       ig      gr
## 1    heart_disease_severity 1.8 0.995 0.99508 0.53907
## 2                      thal 2.0 0.209 0.20946 0.16805
## 3               exer_angina 1.8 0.139 0.13914 0.15264
## 4              exter_angina 1.8 0.139 0.13914 0.15264
## 5                chest_pain 2.5 0.205 0.20502 0.11803
## 6          num_vessels_flour 2.4 0.182 0.18152 0.11577
## 7                     slope 2.2 0.112 0.11242 0.08688
## 8         serum_cholestoral 7.5 0.561 0.56056 0.07956
## 9                    gender 1.8 0.057 0.05725 0.06330
## 10                  oldpeak 4.9 0.249 0.24917 0.06036
## 11           max_heart_rate 6.8 0.334 0.33362 0.05407
## 12  resting_blood_pressure 5.6 0.143 0.14255 0.03024
## 13                      age 5.9 0.137 0.13718 0.02705
## 14           resting_electro 2.1 0.024 0.02415 0.02219
## 15      fasting_blood_sugar 1.6 0.000 0.00046 0.00076
```

Note: It analyzes numerical and categorical variables. It is also used with the numeric discretization method as before, just as `discretize_df`.

[✎Read more here.]

5.2.3.3 `cross_plot`: Distribution plot between input and target variable

Retrieves the relative and absolute distribution between an input and target variable. Useful to explain and report if a variable is important or not.

```
cross_plot(data = heart_disease, input = c("age",
  "oldpeak"), target = "has_heart_disease")
```

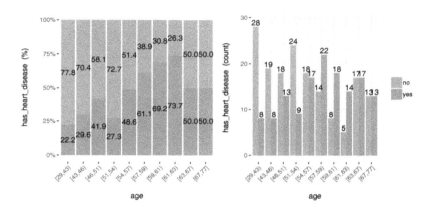

Figure 104: cross plot: visualizing input vs. target variable

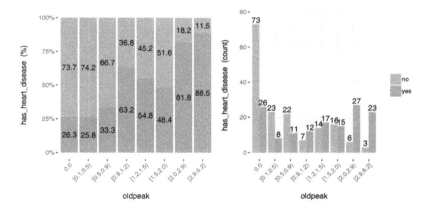

Figure 105: cross plot: visualizing input vs. target variable

Notes:

- `auto_binning`: `TRUE` by default, shows the numerical variable as categorical.
- `path_out` indicates the path directory; if it has a value, then the plot is exported in jpeg.
- `input` can be numeric or categoric, and **target** must be a binary (two-class) variable.
- If `input` is empty, then it runs for all variables.

[⌕Read more here.]

5.2.3.4 plotar: Boxplot and density histogram between input and target variables

Useful to explain and report if a variable is important or not.

Boxplot:

```
plotar(data = heart_disease, input = c("age",
  "oldpeak"), target = "has_heart_disease",
  plot_type = "boxplot")
```

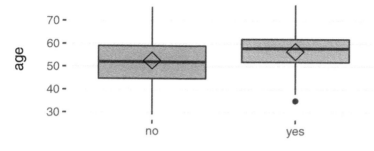

Figure 106: plotar (1): visualizing boxplot

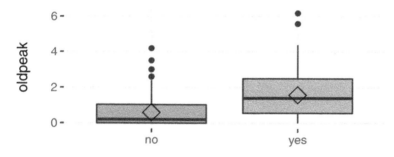

Figure 107: plotar (1): visualizing boxplot

[✎Read more here.]

Density histograms:

```
plotar(data = mtcars, input = "gear", target = "cyl",
    plot_type = "histdens")
```

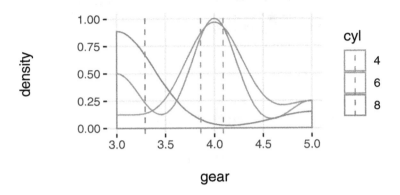

Figure 108: plotar (2): visualizing density histogram

[🔍Read more here.]

Notes:

- `path_out` indicates the path directory; if it has a value, then the plot is exported in jpeg.
- If `input` is empty, then it runs for all numeric variables (skipping the categorical ones).
- `input` must be numeric and target must be categoric.
- `target` can be multi-class (not only binary).

5.2.3.5 `categ_analysis`: Quantitative analysis for binary outcome

Profile a binary target based on a categorical input variable, the representativeness (`perc_rows`) and the accuracy (`perc_target`) for

each value of the input variable; for example, the rate of flu infection
per country.

```
df_ca = categ_analysis(data = data_country,
  input = "country", target = "has_flu")
```

```
head(df_ca)
```

```
##              country mean_target sum_target perc_target
## 1          Malaysia        1.00          1       0.012
## 2            Mexico        0.67          2       0.024
## 3          Portugal        0.20          1       0.012
## 4 United Kingdom        0.18          8       0.096
## 5           Uruguay        0.17         11       0.133
## 6            Israel        0.17          1       0.012
##    q_rows perc_rows
## 1       1     0.001
## 2       3     0.003
## 3       5     0.005
## 4      45     0.049
## 5      63     0.069
## 6       6     0.007
```

Note:

- input variable must be categorical.
- target variable must be binary (two-value).

This function is used to analyze data when we need to reduce variable
cardinality in predictive modeling.

[⚲Read more here.]

5.2.4 Data preparation

5.2.4.1 Data discretization

5.2.4.1.1 `discretize_get_bins` + `discretize_df`: Convert numeric variables to categoric

We need two functions: `discretize_get_bins`, which returns the thresholds for each variable, and then `discretize_df`, which takes the result from the first function and converts the desired variables. The binning criterion is equal frequency.

Example converting only two variables from a dataset.

```
# Step 1: Getting the thresholds for the desired
# variables: 'max_heart_rate' and 'oldpeak'
d_bins = discretize_get_bins(data = heart_disease,
  input = c("max_heart_rate", "oldpeak"), n_bins = 5)
```

```
## [1] "Variables processed: max_heart_rate, oldpeak"
```

```
# Step 2: Applying the threshold to get the final
# processed data frame
heart_disease_discretized =
  discretize_df(data=heart_disease,
                data_bins=d_bins,
                stringsAsFactors=T
                )
```

```
## [1] "Variables processed: max_heart_rate, oldpeak"
```

The following image illustrates the result. Please note that the variable name remains the same.

max_heart_rate_before	max_heart_rate_after	oldpeak_before	oldpeak_after
<int>	<fctr>	<dbl>	<fctr>
171	[171, Inf]	NA	NA.
114	[-Inf, 131)	NA	NA.
151	[147, 160)	1.8	[1.1, 2.0)
160	[160, 171)	1.4	[1.1, 2.0)
158	[147, 160)	0.0	[-Inf, 0.1)
161	[160, 171)	0.5	[0.3, 1.1)

Figure 109: Results of the automatic discretization process

Notes:

- This two-step procedure is thought to be used in production with new data.
- Min and max values for each bin will be -Inf and Inf, respectively.
- A fix in the latest funModeling release (1.6.7) may change the output in certain scenarios. Please check the results if you were using version 1.6.6. More info about this change here[55].

[⟲Read more here.]

5.2.4.2 convert_df_to_categoric: Convert every column in a data frame to character variables

Binning, or discretization criterion for any numerical variable is equal frequency. Factor variables are directly converted to character variables.

```
iris_char = convert_df_to_categoric(data = iris,
  n_bins = 5)
```

```
# checking first rows
head(iris_char)
```

---

[55]https://s3.amazonaws.com/datascienceheroes.com/img/blog/changes_discretize_df.png

297

5.2.4.3 equal_freq: Convert numeric variable to categoric

Converts numeric vector into a factor using the equal frequency criterion.

```
new_age = equal_freq(heart_disease$age, n_bins = 5)
```

```
# checking results
Hmisc::describe(new_age)
```

```
## new_age
##           n  missing distinct
##         303        0        5
##
## Value      [29,46) [46,54) [54,59) [59,63) [63,77]
## Frequency       63      64      71      45      60
## Proportion    0.21    0.21    0.23    0.15    0.20
```

[🔍Read more here.]

Notes:

- Unlike `discretize_get_bins`, this function doesn't insert `-Inf` and `Inf` as the min and max value respectively.

5.2.4.4 range01: Scales variable into the 0 to 1 range

Convert a numeric vector into a scale from 0 to 1 with 0 as the minimum and 1 as the maximum.

```
age_scaled = range01(heart_disease$oldpeak)
```

```
# checking results
summary(age_scaled)
```

```
##    Min. 1st Qu.  Median    Mean 3rd Qu.    Max.
```

```
##    0.00    0.00    0.13    0.17    0.26    1.00
```

5.2.5   Outliers data preparation

5.2.5.1   `hampel_outlier` and `tukey_outlier`:   Gets outliers threshold

Both functions retrieve a two-value vector that indicates the thresholds for which the values are considered as outliers.   The functions `tukey_outlier` and `hampel_outlier` are used internally in `prep_outliers`.

Using Tukey's method:

```
tukey_outlier(heart_disease$resting_blood_pressure)
```

```
## bottom_threshold    top_threshold
##               60              200
```

[⌕Read more here.]

Using Hampel's method:

```
hampel_outlier(heart_disease$resting_blood_pressure)
```

```
## bottom_threshold    top_threshold
##               86              174
```

[⌕Read more here.]

5.2.5.2   `prep_outliers`: Prepare outliers in a data frame

Takes a data frame and returns the same data frame plus the transformations specified in the `input` parameter. It also works with a single vector.

Example considering two variables as input:

```
# Get threshold according to Hampel's method
hampel_outlier(heart_disease$max_heart_rate)

## bottom_threshold     top_threshold
##               86                 220
# Apply function to stop outliers at the threshold values
data_prep = prep_outliers(data = heart_disease,
  input = c("max_heart_rate", "resting_blood_pressure"),
  method = "hampel", type = "stop")
```

Checking the before and after for variable `max_heart_rate`:

```
## [1] "Before transformation -> Min: 71; Max: 202"
```

```
## [1] "After transformation -> Min: 86.283; Max: 202"
```

The min value changed from 71 to 86.23, while the max value remains the same at 202.

Notes:

- `method` can be: `bottom_top`, `tukey` or `hampel`.
- `type` can be: `stop` or `set_na`. If `stop` all values flagged as outliers will be set to the threshold. If `set_na`, then the flagged values will set to `NA`.

[🔍Read more here.]

5.2.6 Predictive model performance

5.2.6.1 gain_lift: Gain and lift performance curve

After computing the scores or probabilities for the class we want to predict, we pass it to the `gain_lift` function, which returns a data frame with performance metrics.

```
# Create machine learning model and get its scores for
# positive case
fit_glm = glm(has_heart_disease ~ age + oldpeak,
  data = heart_disease, family = binomial)
heart_disease$score = predict(fit_glm,
  newdata = heart_disease, type = "response")

# Calculate performance metrics
gain_lift(data = heart_disease, score = "score",
  target = "has_heart_disease")
```

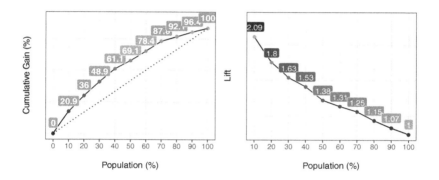

Figure 110: gain lift: visualizing predictive model performance

##	Population	Gain	Lift	Score.Point
## 1	10	21	2.1	0.82
## 2	20	36	1.8	0.70
## 3	30	49	1.6	0.57
## 4	40	61	1.5	0.49
## 5	50	69	1.4	0.40
## 6	60	78	1.3	0.33
## 7	70	88	1.2	0.29
## 8	80	92	1.1	0.25

```
## 9            90    96   1.1        0.20
## 10          100   100   1.0        0.12
```

[🔍Read more here.]

References

Amatriain, Xavier. 2015. "In Machine Learning, What Is Better: More Data or Better Algorithms." http://www.kdnuggets.com/2015/06/machine-learning-more-data-better-algorithms.html.

Caban, Jesus J., Ulas Bagci, Alem Mehari, Shoaib Alam, Joseph R. Fontana, Gregory J. Kato, and Daniel J. Mollura. 2012. "Characterizing Non-Linear Dependencies Among Pairs of Clinical Variables and Imaging Data." *Conf Proc IEEE Eng Med Biol Soc* 2012 (August): 2700–2703. doi:10.1109/EMBC.2012.6346521[56].

Fernandez-Delgado, Manuel. 2014. "Do We Need Hundreds of Classifiers to Solve Real World Classification Problems?" http://jmlr.csail.mit.edu/papers/volume15/delgado14a/delgado14a.pdf.

Fortmann, Scott. 2012. "Understanding the Bias-Variance Tradeoff." http://scott.fortmann-roe.com/docs/BiasVariance.html.

Handbook, Engineering Statistics. 2013. "Measures of Skewness and Kurtosis." http://www.itl.nist.gov/div898/handbook/eda/section3/

---

[56]https://doi.org/10.1109/EMBC.2012.6346521

eda35b.htm.

Hyndman, Rob J. 2010. "Why Every Statistician Should Know About Cross-Validation?" https://robjhyndman.com/hyndsight/crossvalidation/.

———. 2017. "ARIMA Modelling in R." https://www.otexts.org/fpp/8/.

Izbicki, Mike. 2011. "Converting Images into Time Series for Data Mining." https://izbicki.me/blog/converting-images-into-time-series-for-data-mining.html.

Kuhn, Max. 2017. "Recursive Feature Elimination in R Package Caret." https://topepo.github.io/caret/recursive-feature-elimination.html.

McNeese, Bill. 2016. "Are the Skewness and Kurtosis Useful Statistics?" https://www.spcforexcel.com/knowledge/basic-statistics/are-skewness-and-kurtosis-useful-statistics.

Raschka, Sebastian. 2017. "Machine Learning Faq." http://sebastianraschka.com/faq/docs/evaluate-a-model.html.

Reshef, David N., Yakir A. Reshef, Hilary K. Finucane, Sharon R. Grossman, Gilean McVean, Peter J. Turnbaugh, Eric S. Lander, Michael Mitzenmacher, and Pardis C. Sabeti. 2011. "Detecting Novel Associations in Large Data Sets." *Science* 334 (6062): 1518–24. doi:10.1126/science.1205438[57].

stackoverflow.com. 2017. "What Is Entropy and Information Gain?" http://stackoverflow.com/questions/1859554/what-is-entropy-and-information-gain.

stats.stackexchange.com. 2015. "Gradient Boosting Machine Vs Random Forest." https://stats.stackexchange.com/questions/173390/

---

[57]https://doi.org/10.1126/science.1205438

gradient-boosting-tree-vs-random-forest.

———. 2017a. "How to Interpret Mean Decrease in Accuracy and Mean Decrease Gini in Random Forest Models." http://stats.stackexchange.com/questions/197827/how-to-interpret-mean-decrease-in-accuracy-and-mean-decrease-gini-in-random-fore.

———. 2017b. "Percentile Vs Quantile Vs Quartile." https://stats.stackexchange.com/questions/156778/percentile-vs-quantile-vs-quartile.

Suisse, Credit. 2013. "Global Wealth Report 2013." https://publications.credit-suisse.com/tasks/render/file/?fileID=BCDB1364-A105-0560-1332EC9100FF5C83.

Wikipedia. 2017a. "Distribution of Wealth." https://en.wikipedia.org/wiki/Distribution_of_wealth.

———. 2017b. "Monotonic Function." https://en.wikipedia.org/wiki/Monotonic_function.

———. 2017c. "Occam's Razor." https://en.wikipedia.org/wiki/Occam's_razor#Probability_theory_and_statistics.

———. 2017d. "White Noise - Time Series Analysis and Regression." https://en.wikipedia.org/wiki/White_noise.

www.ingramcontent.com/pod-product-compliance
Lightning Source LLC
LaVergne TN
LVHW042123070326
832902LV00036B/568